SOUTH SEA TALES

Jack London

DOVER PUBLICATIONS, INC.
Mineola, New York

Bibliographical Note

This Dover edition, first published in 2001, is an unabridged, unaltered republication of the work published in 1911 by The Macmillan Company. The text was first published, in serial form, in 1907.

Library of Congress Cataloging-in-Publication Data

London, Jack, 1876–1916.
    South Sea tales / Jack London.
        p. cm.
    Contents: The house of Mapuhi—The whale tooth—Mauki—Yah! Yah! Yah!—The heathen—The terrible Solomons—The inevitable white man—The seed of McCoy.
        ISBN-13: 978-0-486-41912-1 (pbk.)
        ISBN-10: 0-486-41912-6 (pbk.)
        1. Oceania—Fiction. I. Title.

PS3523.O46 S76 2001
813'.52—dc21

                                                                                                2001028589

Manufactured in the United States by LSC Communications
41912605   2017
www.doverpublications.com

Contents

The House of Mapuhi

Despite the heavy clumsiness of her lines, the *Aorai* handled easily in the light breeze, and her captain ran her well in before he hove to just outside the suck of the surf. The atoll of Hikueru lay low on the water, a circle of pounded coral sand a hundred yards wide, twenty miles in circumference, and from three to five feet above high-water mark. On the bottom of the huge and glassy lagoon was much pearl shell, and from the deck of the schooner, across the slender ring of the atoll, the divers could be seen at work. But the lagoon had no entrance for even a trading schooner. With a favoring breeze cutters could win in through the tortuous and shallow channel, but the schooners lay off and on outside and sent in their small boats.

The *Aorai* swung out a boat smartly, into which sprang half a dozen brown-skinned sailors clad only in scarlet loincloths. They took the oars, while in the stern-sheets, at the steering sweep, stood a young man garbed in the tropic white that marks the European. But he was not all European. The golden strain of Polynesia betrayed itself in the sun-gilt of his fair skin and cast up golden sheens and lights through the glimmering blue of his eyes. Raoul he was, Alexandré Raoul, youngest son of Marie Raoul, the wealthy quarter-caste, who owned and managed half a dozen trading schooners similar to the *Aorai*. Across an eddy just outside the entrance, and in and through and over a boiling tide-rip, the boat fought its way to the mirrored calm of the lagoon. Young Raoul leaped out upon the white sand and shook hands with a tall native. The man's chest and shoulders were magnificent, but the stump of a right arm, beyond the flesh of

1

which the age-whitened bone projected several inches, attested the encounter with a shark that had put an end to his diving days and made him a fawner and an intriguer for small favors.

"Have you heard, Alec?" were his first words. "Mapuhi has found a pearl—such a pearl. Never was there one like it ever fished up in Hikueru, nor in all the Paumotus, nor in all the world. Buy it from him. He has it now. And remember that I told you first. He is a fool and you can get it cheap. Have you any tobacco?"

Straight up the beach to a shack under a pandanus-tree Raoul headed. He was his mother's supercargo, and his business was to comb all the Paumotus for the wealth of copra, shell, and pearls that they yielded up.

He was a young supercargo, it was his second voyage in such capacity, and he suffered much secret worry from his lack of experience in pricing pearls. But when Mapuhi exposed the pearl to his sight he managed to suppress the startle it gave him, and to maintain a careless, commercial expression on his face. For the pearl had struck him a blow. It was large as a pigeon egg, a perfect sphere, of a whiteness that reflected opalescent lights from all colors about it. It was alive. Never had he seen anything like it. When Mapuhi dropped it into his hand he was surprised by the weight of it. That showed that it was a good pearl. He examined it closely, through a pocket magnifying-glass. It was without flaw or blemish. The purity of it seemed almost to melt into the atmosphere out of his hand. In the shade it was softly luminous, gleaming like a tender moon. So translucently white was it, that when he dropped it into a glass of water he had difficulty in finding it. So straight and swiftly had it sunk to the bottom that he knew its weight was excellent.

"Well, what do you want for it?" he asked, with a fine assumption of nonchalance.

"I want—" Mapuhi began, and behind him, framing his own dark face, the dark faces of two women and a girl nodded concurrence in what he wanted. Their heads were bent forward, they were animated by a suppressed eagerness, their eyes flashed avariciously.

"I want a house," Mapuhi went on. "It must have a roof of galvanized iron and an octagon-drop-clock. It must be six fathoms long with a porch all around. A big room must be in the centre, with a round table in the middle of it and the octagon-drop-clock on the wall. There must be four bedrooms, two on each side of the big room, and in each bedroom must be an iron bed, two chairs, and a washstand. And back of the house must be a kitchen, a good kitchen, with pots and pans and a stove. And you must build the house on my island, which is Fakarava."

"Is that all?" Raoul asked incredulously.

"There must be a sewing-machine," spoke up Tefara, Mapuhi's wife.

"Not forgetting the octagon-drop-clock," added Nauri, Mapuhi's mother.

"Yes, that is all," said Mapuhi.

Young Raoul laughed. He laughed long and heartily. But while he laughed he secretly performed problems in mental arithmetic. He had never built a house in his life, and his notions concerning house building were hazy. While he laughed, he calculated the cost of the voyage to Tahiti for materials, of the materials themselves, of the voyage back again to Fakarava, and the cost of landing the materials and of building the house. It would come to four thousand French dollars, allowing a margin for safety—four thousand French dollars were equivalent to twenty thousand francs. It was impossible. How was he to know the value of such a pearl? Twenty thousand francs was a lot of money—and of his mother's money at that.

"Mapuhi," he said, "you are a big fool. Set a money price."

But Mapuhi shook his head, and the three heads behind him shook with his.

"I want the house," he said. "It must be six fathoms long with a porch all around—"

"Yes, yes," Raoul interrupted. "I know all about your house, but it won't do. I'll give you a thousand Chili dollars."

The four heads chorused a silent negative.

"And a hundred Chili dollars in trade."

"I want the house," Mapuhi began.

"What good will the house do you?" Raoul demanded. "The

first hurricane that comes along will wash it away. You ought to know. Captain Raffy says it looks like a hurricane right now."

"Not on Fakarava," said Mapuhi. "The land is much higher there. On this island, yes. Any hurricane can sweep Hikueru. I will have the house on Fakarava. It must be six fathoms long with a porch all around—"

And Raoul listened again to the tale of the house. Several hours he spent in the endeavor to hammer the house-obsession out of Mapuhi's mind; but Mapuhi's mother and wife, and Ngakura, Mapuhi's daughter, bolstered him in his resolve for the house. Through the open doorway, while he listened for the twentieth time to the detailed description of the house that was wanted, Raoul saw his schooner's second boat draw up on the beach. The sailors rested on the oars, advertising haste to be gone. The first mate of the *Aorai* sprang ashore, exchanged a word with the one-armed native, then hurried toward Raoul. The day grew suddenly dark, as a squall obscured the face of the sun. Across the lagoon Raoul could see approaching the ominous line of the puff of wind.

"Captain Raffy says you've got to get to hell outa here," was the mate's greeting. "If there's any shell, we've got to run the risk of picking it up later on—so he says. The barometer's dropped to twenty-nine-seventy."

The gust of wind struck the pandanus-tree overhead and tore through the palms beyond, flinging half a dozen ripe cocoanuts with heavy thuds to the ground. Then came the rain out of the distance, advancing with the roar of a gale of wind and causing the water of the lagoon to smoke in driven windrows. The sharp rattle of the first drops was on the leaves when Raoul sprang to his feet.

"A thousand Chili dollars, cash down, Mapuhi," he said. "And two hundred Chili dollars in trade."

"I want a house—" the other began.

"Mapuhi!" Raoul yelled, in order to make himself heard. "You are a fool!"

He flung out of the house, and, side by side with the mate, fought his way down the beach toward the boat. They could not see the boat. The tropic rain sheeted about them so that they could see only the beach under their feet and the spiteful little waves from the lagoon that snapped and bit at the sand. A figure appeared through the deluge. It was Huru-Huru, the man with the one arm.

"Did you get the pearl?" he yelled in Raoul's ear.

"Mapuhi is a fool!" was the answering yell, and the next moment they were lost to each other in the descending water.

Half an hour later, Huru-Huru, watching from the seaward side of the atoll, saw the two boats hoisted in and the *Aorai* pointing her nose out to sea. And near her, just come in from the sea on the wings of the squall, he saw another schooner hove to and dropping a boat into the water. He knew her. It was the *Orohena*, owned by Toriki, the half-caste trader, who served as his own supercargo and who doubtlessly was even then in the stern-sheets of the boat. Huru-Huru chuckled. He knew that Mapuhi owed Toriki for trade-goods advanced the year before.

The squall had passed. The hot sun was blazing down, and the lagoon was once more a mirror. But the air was sticky like mucilage, and the weight of it seemed to burden the lungs and make breathing difficult.

"Have you heard the news, Toriki?" Huru-Huru asked. "Mapuhi has found a pearl. Never was there a pearl like it ever fished up in Hikueru, nor anywhere in the Paumotus, nor anywhere in all the world. Mapuhi is a fool. Besides, he owes you money. Remember that I told you first. Have you any tobacco?"

And to the grass-shack of Mapuhi went Toriki. He was a masterful man, withal a fairly stupid one. Carelessly he glanced at the wonderful pearl—glanced for a moment only; and carelessly he dropped it into his pocket.

"You are lucky," he said. "It is a nice pearl. I will give you credit on the books."

"I want a house," Mapuhi began, in consternation. "It must be six fathoms—"

"Six fathoms your grandmother!" was the trader's retort. "You want to pay up your debts, that's what you want. You owed me twelve hundred dollars Chili. Very well; you owe them no longer. The amount is squared. Besides, I will give you credit for two hundred Chili. If, when I get to Tahiti, the pearl sells well,

I will give you credit for another hundred—that will make three hundred. But mind, only if the pearl sells well. I may even lose money on it."

Mapuhi folded his arms in sorrow and sat with bowed head. He had been robbed of his pearl. In place of the house, he had paid a debt. There was nothing to show for the pearl.

"You are a fool," said Tefara.

"You are a fool," said Nauri, his mother. "Why did you let the pearl into his hand?"

"What was I to do?" Mapuhi protested. "I owed him the money. He knew I had the pearl. You heard him yourself ask to see it. I had not told him. He knew. Somebody else told him. And I owed him the money."

"Mapuhi is a fool," mimicked Ngakura.

She was twelve years old and did not know any better. Mapuhi relieved his feelings by sending her reeling from a box on the ear; while Tefara and Nauri burst into tears and continued to upbraid him after the manner of women.

Huru-Huru, watching on the beach, saw a third schooner that he knew heave to outside the entrance and drop a boat. It was the *Hira*, well named, for she was owned by Levy, the German Jew, the greatest pearl-buyer of them all, and, as was well known, Hira was the Tahitian god of fishermen and thieves.

"Have you heard the news?" Huru-Huru asked, as Levy, a fat man with massive asymmetrical features, stepped out upon the beach. "Mapuhi has found a pearl. There was never a pearl like it in Hikueru, in all the Paumotus, in all the world. Mapuhi is a fool. He has sold it to Toriki for fourteen hundred Chili—I listened outside and heard. Toriki is likewise a fool. You can buy it from him cheap. Remember that I told you first. Have you any tobacco?"

"Where is Toriki?"

"In the house of Captain Lynch, drinking absinthe. He has been there an hour."

And while Levy and Toriki drank absinthe and chaffered over the pearl, Huru-Huru listened and heard the stupendous price of twenty-five thousand francs agreed upon.

It was at this time that both the *Orohena* and the *Hira*, running in close to the shore, began firing guns and signalling frantically. The three men stepped outside in time to see the two schooners go hastily about and head off shore, dropping mainsails and flying-jibs on the run in the teeth of the squall that heeled them far over on the whitened water. Then the rain blotted them out.

"They'll be back after it's over," said Toriki. "We'd better be getting out of here."

"I reckon the glass has fallen some more," said Captain Lynch.

He was a white-bearded sea-captain, too old for service, who had learned that the only way to live on comfortable terms with his asthma was on Hikueru. He went inside to look at the barometer.

"Great God!" they heard him exclaim, and rushed in to join him at staring at a dial, which marked twenty-nine-twenty.

Again they came out, this time anxiously to consult sea and sky. The squall had cleared away, but the sky remained overcast. The two schooners, under all sail and joined by a third, could be seen making back. A veer in the wind induced them to slack off sheets, and five minutes afterward a sudden veer from the opposite quarter caught all three schooners aback, and those on shore could see the boom-tackles being slacked away or cast off on the jump. The sound of the surf was loud, hollow, and menacing, and a heavy swell was setting in. A terrible sheet of lightning burst before their eyes, illuminating the dark day, and the thunder rolled wildly about them.

Toriki and Levy broke into a run for their boats, the latter ambling along like a panic-stricken hippopotamus. As their two boats swept out the entrance, they passed the boat of the *Aorai* coming in. In the stern-sheets, encouraging the rowers, was Raoul. Unable to shake the vision of the pearl from his mind, he was returning to accept Mapuhi's price of a house.

He landed on the beach in the midst of a driving thunder squall that was so dense that he collided with Huru-Huru before he saw him.

"Too late," yelled Huru-Huru. "Mapuhi sold it to Toriki for fourteen hundred Chili, and Toriki sold it to Levy for twenty-five thousand francs. And Levy will sell it in France for a hundred thousand francs. Have you any tobacco?"

Raoul felt relieved. His troubles about the pearl were over. He need not worry any more, even if he had not got the pearl. But he did not believe Huru-Huru. Mapuhi might well have sold it for fourteen hundred Chili, but that Levy, who knew pearls, should have paid twenty-five thousand francs was too wide a stretch. Raoul decided to interview Captain Lynch on the subject, but when he arrived at that ancient mariner's house, he found him looking wide-eyed at the barometer.

"What do you read it?" Captain Lynch asked anxiously, rubbing his spectacles and staring again at the instrument.

"Twenty-nine-ten," said Raoul. "I have never seen it so low before."

"I should say not!" snorted the captain. "Fifty years boy and man on all the seas, and I've never seen it go down to that. Listen!"

They stood for a moment, while the surf rumbled and shook the house. Then they went outside. The squall had passed. They could see the *Aorai* lying becalmed a mile away and pitching and tossing madly in the tremendous seas that rolled in stately procession down out of the northeast and flung themselves furiously upon the coral shore. One of the sailors from the boat pointed at the mouth of the passage and shook his head. Raoul looked and saw a white anarchy of foam and surge.

"I guess I'll stay with you to-night, Captain," he said; then turned to the sailor and told him to haul the boat out and to find shelter for himself and fellows.

"Twenty-nine flat," Captain Lynch reported, coming out from another look at the barometer, a chair in his hand.

He sat down and stared at the spectacle of the sea. The sun came out, increasing the sultriness of the day, while the dead calm still held. The seas continued to increase in magnitude.

"What makes that sea is what gets me," Raoul muttered petulantly. "There is no wind, yet look at it, look at that fellow there!"

Miles in length, carrying tens of thousands of tons in weight, its impact shook the frail atoll like an earthquake. Captain Lynch was startled.

"Gracious!" he exclaimed, half-rising from his chair, then sinking back.

"But there is no wind," Raoul persisted. "I could understand it if there was wind along with it."

"You'll get the wind soon enough without worryin' for it," was the grim reply.

The two men sat on in silence. The sweat stood out on their skin in myriads of tiny drops that ran together, forming blotches of moisture, which, in turn, coalesced into rivulets that dripped to the ground. They panted for breath, the old man's efforts being especially painful. A sea swept up the beach, licking around the trunks of the cocoanuts and subsiding almost at their feet.

"'Way past high-water mark," Captain Lynch remarked; "and I've been here eleven years." He looked at his watch. "It is three o'clock."

A man and woman, at their heels a motley following of brats and curs, trailed disconsolately by. They came to a halt beyond the house, and, after much irresolution, sat down in the sand. A few minutes later another family trailed in from the opposite direction, the men and women carrying a heterogeneous assortment of possessions. And soon several hundred persons of all ages and sexes were congregated about the captain's dwelling. He called to one new arrival, a woman with a nursing babe in her arms, and in answer received the information that her house had just been swept into the lagoon.

This was the highest spot of land in miles, and already, in many places on either hand, the great seas were making a clean breach of the slender ring of the atoll and surging into the lagoon. Twenty miles around stretched the ring of the atoll, and in no place was it more than fifty fathoms wide. It was the height of the diving season, and from all the islands around, even as far as Tahiti, the natives had gathered.

"There are twelve hundred men, women, and children here," said Captain Lynch. "I wonder how many will be here to-morrow morning."

"But why don't it blow?—that's what I want to know," Raoul demanded.

"Don't worry, young man, don't worry; you'll get your troubles fast enough."

Even as Captain Lynch spoke, a great watery mass smote the atoll. The seawater churned about them three inches deep under their chairs. A low wail of fear went up from the many women. The children, with clasped hands, stared at the immense rollers and cried piteously. Chickens and cats, wading perturbedly in the water, as by common consent, with flight and scramble took refuge on the roof of the captain's house. A Paumotan, with a litter of new-born puppies in a basket, climbed into a cocoanut tree and twenty feet above the ground made the basket fast. The mother floundered about in the water beneath, whining and yelping.

And still the sun shone brightly and the dead calm continued. They sat and watched the seas and the insane pitching of the *Aorai*. Captain Lynch gazed at the huge mountains of water sweeping in until he could gaze no more. He covered his face with his hands to shut out the sight; then went into the house.

"Twenty-eight-sixty," he said quietly when he returned.

In his arm was a coil of small rope. He cut it into two-fathom lengths, giving one to Raoul and, retaining one for himself, distributed the remainder among the women with the advice to pick out a tree and climb.

A light air began to blow out of the northeast, and the fan of it on his cheek seemed to cheer Raoul up. He could see the *Aorai* trimming her sheets and heading off shore, and he regretted that he was not on her. She would get away at any rate, but as for the atoll— A sea breached across, almost sweeping him off his feet, and he selected a tree. Then he remembered the barometer and ran back to the house. He encountered Captain Lynch on the same errand and together they went in.

"Twenty-eight-twenty," said the old mariner. "It's going to be fair hell around here—what was that?"

The air seemed filled with the rush of something. The house quivered and vibrated, and they heard the thrumming of a mighty note of sound. The windows rattled. Two panes crashed; a draught of wind tore in, striking them and making them stagger. The door opposite banged shut, shattering the latch. The white doorknob crumbled in fragments to the floor. The room's walls bulged like a gas balloon in the process of sudden inflation. Then came a new sound like the rattle of musketry, as the spray from a sea struck the wall of the house. Captain Lynch looked at his watch. It was four o'clock. He put on a coat of pilot cloth, unhooked the barometer, and stowed it away in a capacious pocket. Again a sea struck the house, with a heavy thud, and the light building tilted, twisted quarter-around on its foundation, and sank down, its floor at an angle of ten degrees.

Raoul went out first. The wind caught him and whirled him away. He noted that it had hauled around to the east. With a great effort he threw himself on the sand, crouching and holding his own. Captain Lynch, driven like a wisp of straw, sprawled over him. Two of the *Aorai's* sailors, leaving a cocoanut tree to which they had been clinging, came to their aid, leaning against the wind at impossible angles and fighting and clawing every inch of the way.

The old man's joints were stiff and he could not climb, so the sailors, by means of short ends of rope tied together, hoisted him up the trunk, a few feet at a time, till they could make him fast, at the top of the tree, fifty feet from the ground. Raoul passed his length of rope around the base of an adjacent tree and stood looking on. The wind was frightful. He had never dreamed it could blow so hard. A sea breached across the atoll, wetting him to the knees ere it subsided into the lagoon. The sun had disappeared, and a lead-colored twilight settled down. A few drops of rain, driving horizontally, struck him. The impact was like that of leaden pellets. A splash of salt spray struck his face. It was like the slap of a man's hand. His cheeks stung, and involuntary tears of pain were in his smarting eyes. Several hundred natives had taken to the trees, and he could have laughed at the bunches of human fruit clustering in the tops. Then, being Tahitian-born, he doubled his body at the waist, clasped the trunk of his tree with his hands, pressed the soles of his feet against the near surface of the trunk, and began to walk up the tree. At the top he found two women, two children, and a man. One little girl clasped a housecat in her arms.

From his eyrie he waved his hand to Captain Lynch, and that

doughty patriarch waved back. Raoul was appalled at the sky. It had approached much nearer—in fact, it seemed just over his head; and it had turned from lead to black. Many people were still on the ground grouped about the bases of the trees and holding on. Several such clusters were praying, and in one the Mormon missionary was exhorting. A weird sound, rhythmical, faint as the faintest chirp of a far cricket, enduring but for a moment, but in that moment suggesting to him vaguely the thought of heaven and celestial music, came to his ear. He glanced about him and saw, at the base of another tree, a large cluster of people holding on by ropes and by one another. He could see their faces working and their lips moving in unison. No sound came to him, but he knew that they were singing hymns.

Still the wind continued to blow harder. By no conscious process could he measure it, for it had long since passed beyond all his experience of wind; but he knew somehow, nevertheless, that it was blowing harder. Not far away a tree was uprooted, flinging its load of human beings to the ground. A sea washed across the strip of sand, and they were gone. Things were happening quickly. He saw a brown shoulder and a black head silhouetted against the churning white of the lagoon. The next instant that, too, had vanished. Other trees were going, falling and crisscrossing like matches. He was amazed at the power of the wind. His own tree was swaying perilously, one woman was wailing and clutching the little girl, who in turn still hung on to the cat.

The man, holding the other child, touched Raoul's arm and pointed. He looked and saw the Mormon church careering drunkenly a hundred feet away. It had been torn from its foundations, and wind and sea were heaving and shoving it toward the lagoon. A frightful wall of water caught it, tilted it, and flung it against half a dozen cocoanut trees. The bunches of human fruit fell like ripe cocoanuts. The subsiding wave showed them on the ground, some lying motionless, others squirming and writhing. They reminded him strangely of ants. He was not shocked. He had risen above horror. Quite as a matter of course he noted the succeeding wave sweep the sand clean of the human wreckage. A third wave, more colossal than any he had yet seen, hurled the church into the lagoon, where it floated off into the obscurity to leeward, half-submerged, reminding him for all the world of a Noah's ark.

He looked for Captain Lynch's house, and was surprised to find it gone. Things certainly were happening quickly. He noticed that many of the people in the trees that still held had descended to the ground. The wind had yet again increased. His own tree showed that. It no longer swayed or bent over and back. Instead, it remained practically stationary, curved in a rigid angle from the wind and merely vibrating. But the vibration was sickening. It was like that of a tuning-fork or the tongue of a jew's-harp. It was the rapidity of the vibration that made it so bad. Even though its roots held, it could not stand the strain for long. Something would have to break.

Ah, there was one that had gone. He had not seen it go, but there it stood, the remnant, broken off half-way up the trunk. One did not know what happened unless he saw it. The mere crashing of trees and wails of human despair occupied no place in that mighty volume of sound. He chanced to be looking in Captain Lynch's direction when it happened. He saw the trunk of the tree, half-way up, splinter and part without noise. The head of the tree, with three sailors of the *Aorai* and the old captain, sailed off over the lagoon. It did not fall to the ground, but drove through the air like a piece of chaff. For a hundred yards he followed its flight, when it struck the water. He strained his eyes, and was sure that he saw Captain Lynch wave farewell.

Raoul did not wait for anything more. He touched the native and made signs to descend to the ground. The man was willing, but his women were paralyzed from terror, and he elected to remain with them. Raoul passed his rope around the tree and slid down. A rush of salt water went over his head. He held his breath and clung desperately to the rope. The water subsided, and in the shelter of the trunk he breathed once more. He fastened the rope more securely, and then was put under by another sea. One of the women slid down and joined him, the native remaining by the other woman, the two children, and the cat.

The supercargo had noticed how the groups clinging at the

bases of the other trees continually diminished. Now he saw the process work out alongside him. It required all his strength to hold on, and the woman who had joined him was growing weaker. Each time he emerged from a sea he was surprised to find himself still there, and next, surprised to find the woman still there. At last he emerged to find himself alone. He looked up. The top of the tree had gone as well. At half its original height, a splintered end vibrated. He was safe. The roots still held, while the tree had been shorn of its windage. He began to climb up. He was so weak that he went slowly, and sea after sea caught him before he was above them. Then he tied himself to the trunk and stiffened his soul to face the night and he knew not what.

He felt very lonely in the darkness. At times it seemed to him that it was the end of the world and that he was the last one left alive. Still the wind increased. Hour after hour it increased. By what he calculated was eleven o'clock, the wind had become unbelievable. It was a horrible, monstrous thing, a screaming fury, a wall that smote and passed on but that continued to smite and pass on—a wall without end. It seemed to him that he had become light and ethereal; that it was he that was in motion; that he was being driven with inconceivable velocity through unending solidness. The wind was no longer air in motion. It had become substantial as water or quicksilver. He had a feeling that he could reach into it and tear it out in chunks as one might do with the meat in the carcass of a steer; that he could seize hold of the wind and hang on to it as a man might hang on to the face of a cliff.

The wind strangled him. He could not face it and breathe, for it rushed in through his mouth and nostrils, distending his lungs like bladders. At such moments it seemed to him that his body was being packed and swollen with solid earth. Only by pressing his lips to the trunk of the tree could he breathe. Also, the ceaseless impact of the wind exhausted him. Body and brain became wearied. He no longer observed, no longer thought, and was but semiconscious. One idea constituted his consciousness: *So this was a hurricane.* That one idea persisted irregularly. It was like a feeble flame that flickered occasionally. From a state of stupor he would return to it—*So this was a hurricane.* Then he would go off into another stupor.

The height of the hurricane endured from eleven at night till three in the morning, and it was at eleven that the tree in which clung Mapuhi and his women snapped off. Mapuhi rose to the surface of the lagoon, still clutching his daughter Ngakura. Only a South Sea islander could have lived in such a driving smother. The pandanus-tree, to which he attached himself, turned over and over in the froth and churn; and it was only by holding on at times and waiting, and at other times shifting his grips rapidly, that he was able to get his head and Ngakura's to the surface at intervals sufficiently near together to keep the breath in them. But the air was mostly water, what with flying spray and sheeted rain that poured along at right angles to the perpendicular.

It was ten miles across the lagoon to the farther ring of sand. Here, tossing tree-trunks, timbers, wrecks of cutters, and wreckage of houses, killed nine out of ten of the miserable beings who survived the passage of the lagoon. Half-drowned, exhausted, they were hurled into this mad mortar of the elements and battered into formless flesh. But Mapuhi was fortunate. His chance was the one in ten; it fell to him by the freakage of fate. He emerged upon the sand, bleeding from a score of wounds. Ngakura's left arm was broken; the fingers of her right hand were crushed; and cheek and forehead were laid open to the bone. He clutched a tree that yet stood, and clung on, holding the girl and sobbing for air, while the waters of the lagoon washed by knee-high and at times waist-high.

At three in the morning the backbone of the hurricane broke. By five no more than a stiff breeze was blowing. And by six it was dead calm and the sun was shining. The sea had gone down. On the yet restless edge of the lagoon, Mapuhi saw the broken bodies of those that had failed in the landing. Undoubtedly Tefara and Nauri were among them. He went along the beach examining them, and came upon his wife, lying half in and half out of the water. He sat down and wept, making harsh animal-noises after the manner of primitive grief. Then she stirred uneasily, and groaned. He looked more closely. Not only was she alive, but she was uninjured. She was merely sleeping. Hers also had been the one chance in ten.

Of the twelve hundred alive the night before but three hundred remained. The Mormon missionary and a gendarme made the census. The lagoon was cluttered with corpses. Not a house nor a hut was standing. In the whole atoll not two stones remained one upon another. One in fifty of the cocoanut palms still stood, and they were wrecks, while on not one of them remained a single nut. There was no fresh water. The shallow wells that caught the surface seepage of the rain were filled with salt. Out of the lagoon a few soaked bags of flour were recovered. The survivors cut the hearts out of the fallen cocoanut trees and ate them. Here and there they crawled into tiny hutches, made by hollowing out the sand and covering over with fragments of metal roofing. The missionary made a crude still, but he could not distill water for three hundred persons. By the end of the second day, Raoul, taking a bath in the lagoon, discovered that his thirst was somewhat relieved. He cried out the news, and thereupon three hundred men, women, and children could have been seen, standing up to their necks in the lagoon and trying to drink water in through their skins. Their dead floated about them, or were stepped upon where they still lay upon the bottom. On the third day the people buried their dead and sat down to wait for the rescue steamers.

In the meantime, Nauri, torn from her family by the hurricane, had been swept away on an adventure of her own. Clinging to a rough plank that wounded and bruised her and that filled her body with splinters, she was thrown clear over the atoll and carried away to sea. Here, under the amazing buffets of mountains of water, she lost her plank. She was an old woman nearly sixty; but she was Paumotan-born, and she had never been out of sight of the sea in her life. Swimming in the darkness, strangling, suffocating, fighting for air, she was struck a heavy blow on the shoulder by a cocoanut. On the instant her plan was formed, and she seized the nut. In the next hour she captured seven more. Tied together, they formed a life-buoy that preserved her life while at the same time it threatened to pound her to a jelly. She was a fat woman, and she bruised easily; but she had had experience of hurricanes, and, while she prayed to her shark god for protection from sharks, she waited for the wind to break. But at three o'clock she was in such a stupor that she did not know. Nor did she know at six o'clock when the dead calm settled down. She was shocked into consciousness when she was thrown upon the sand. She dug in with raw and bleeding hands and feet and clawed against the backwash until she was beyond the reach of the waves.

She knew where she was. This land could be no other than the tiny islet of Takokota. It had no lagoon. No one lived upon it. Hikueru was fifteen miles away. She could not see Hikueru, but she knew that it lay to the south. The days went by, and she lived on the cocoanuts that had kept her afloat. They supplied her with drinking water and with food. But she did not drink all she wanted, nor eat all she wanted. Rescue was problematical. She saw the smoke of the rescue steamers on the horizon, but what steamer could be expected to come to lonely, uninhabited Takokota?

From the first she was tormented by corpses. The sea persisted in flinging them upon her bit of sand, and she persisted, until her strength failed, in thrusting them back into the sea where the sharks tore at them and devoured them. When her strength failed, the bodies festooned her beach with ghastly horror, and she withdrew from them as far as she could, which was not far.

By the tenth day her last cocoanut was gone, and she was shrivelling from thirst. She dragged herself along the sand, looking for cocoanuts. It was strange that so many bodies floated up, and no nuts. Surely, there were more cocoanuts afloat than dead men! She gave up at last, and lay exhausted. The end had come. Nothing remained but to wait for death.

Coming out of a stupor, she became slowly aware that she was gazing at a patch of sandy-red hair on the head of a corpse. The sea flung the body toward her, then drew it back. It turned over, and she saw that it had no face. Yet there was something familiar about that patch of sandy-red hair. An hour passed. She did not exert herself to make the identification. She was waiting to

die, and it mattered little to her what man that thing of horror
once might have been.

But at the end of the hour she sat up slowly and stared at the
corpse. An unusually large wave had thrown it beyond the reach
of the lesser waves. Yes, she was right; that patch of red hair
could belong to but one man in the Paumotus. It was Levy, the
German Jew, the man who had bought the pearl and carried it
away on the *Hira*. Well, one thing was evident: the *Hira* had
been lost. The pearl-buyer's god of fishermen and thieves had
gone back on him.

She crawled down to the dead man. His shirt had been torn
away, and she could see the leather money-belt about his waist.
She held her breath and tugged at the buckles. They gave
easier than she had expected, and she crawled hurriedly away
across the sand, dragging the belt after her. Pocket after pocket
she unbuckled in the belt and found empty. Where could he
have put it? In the last pocket of all she found it, the first and
only pearl he had bought on the voyage. She crawled a few feet
farther, to escape the pestilence of the belt, and examined the
pearl. It was the one Mapuhi had found and been robbed of by
Toriki. She weighed it in her hand and rolled it back and forth
caressingly. But in it she saw no intrinsic beauty. What she did
see was the house Mapuhi and Tefara and she had builded so
carefully in their minds. Each time she looked at the pearl she
saw the house in all its details, including the octagon-drop-clock
on the wall. That was something to live for.

She tore a strip from her *ahu* and tied the pearl securely
about her neck. Then she went on along the beach, panting and
groaning, but resolutely seeking for cocoanuts. Quickly she
found one, and, as she glanced around, a second. She broke one,
drinking its water, which was mildewy, and eating the last parti-
cle of the meat. A little later she found a shattered dugout. Its
outrigger was gone, but she was hopeful, and, before the day
was out, she found the outrigger. Every find was an augury. The
pearl was a talisman. Late in the afternoon she saw a wooden
box floating low in the water. When she dragged it out on the
beach its contents rattled, and inside she found ten tins of
salmon. She opened one by hammering it on the canoe. When

a leak was started, she drained the tin. After that she spent several hours in extracting the salmon, hammering and squeezing it out a morsel at a time.

Eight days longer she waited for rescue. In the meantime she fastened the outrigger back on the canoe, using for lashings all the cocoanut-fibre she could find, and also what remained of her *ahu*. The canoe was badly cracked, and she could not make it water-tight; but a calabash made from a cocoanut she stored on board for a bailer. She was hard put for a paddle. With a piece of tin she sawed off all her hair close to the scalp. Out of the hair she braided a cord; and by means of the cord she lashed a three-foot piece of broom-handle to a board from the salmon case. She gnawed wedges with her teeth and with them wedged the lashing.

On the eighteenth day, at midnight, she launched the canoe through the surf and started back for Hikueru. She was an old woman. Hardship had stripped her fat from her till scarcely more than bones and skin and a few stringy muscles remained. The canoe was large and should have been paddled by three strong men. But she did it alone, with a make-shift paddle. Also, the canoe leaked badly, and one-third of her time was devoted to bailing. By clear daylight she looked vainly for Hikueru. Astern, Takokota had sunk beneath the sea-rim. The sun blazed down on her nakedness, compelling her body to surrender its moisture. Two tins of salmon were left, and in the course of the day she battered holes in them and drained the liquid. She had no time to waste in extracting the meat. A current was setting to the westward, she made westing whether she made southing or not.

In the early afternoon, standing upright in the canoe, she sighted Hikueru. Its wealth of cocoanut palms was gone. Only here and there, at wide intervals, could she see the ragged remnants of trees. The sight cheered her. She was nearer than she had thought. The current was setting her to the westward. She bore up against it and paddled on. The wedges in the paddle-lashing worked loose, and she lost much time, at frequent intervals, in driving them tight. Then there was the bailing. One hour in three she had to cease paddling in order to bail. And all the time she drifted to the westward.

By sunset Hikueru bore southeast from her, three miles away. There was a full moon, and by eight o'clock the land was due east and two miles away. She struggled on for another hour, but the land was as far away as ever. She was in the main grip of the current; the canoe was too large; the paddle was too inadequate; and too much of her time and strength was wasted in bailing. Besides, she was very weak and growing weaker. Despite her efforts, the canoe was drifting off to the westward.

She breathed a prayer to her shark god, slipped over the side, and began to swim. She was actually refreshed by the water, and quickly left the canoe astern. At the end of an hour the land was perceptibly nearer. Then came her fright. Right before her eyes, not twenty feet away, a large fin cut the water. She swam steadily toward it, and slowly it glided away, curving off toward the right and circling around her. She kept her eyes on the fin and swam on. When the fin disappeared, she lay face downward on the water and watched. When the fin reappeared she resumed her swimming. The monster was lazy—she could see that. Without doubt he had been well fed since the hurricane. Had he been very hungry, she knew he would not have hesitated from making a dash for her. He was fifteen feet long, and one bite, she knew, could cut her in half.

But she did not have any time to waste on him. Whether she swam or not, the current drew away from the land just the same. A half-hour went by, and the shark began to grow bolder. Seeing no harm in her he drew closer, in narrowing circles, cocking his eyes at her impudently as he slid past. Sooner or later, she knew well enough, he would get up sufficient courage to dash at her. She resolved to play first. It was a desperate act she meditated. She was an old woman, alone in the sea and weak from starvation and hardship; and yet she, in the face of this sea-tiger, must anticipate his dash by herself dashing at him. She swam on, waiting her chance. At last he passed languidly by, barely eight feet away. She rushed at him suddenly, feigning that she was attacking him. He gave a wild flirt of his tail as he fled away, and his sandpaper hide, striking her, took off her skin from elbow to shoulder. He swam rapidly, in a widening circle, and at last disappeared.

In the hole in the sand, covered over by fragments of metal roofing, Mapuhi and Tefara lay disputing.

"If you had done as I said," charged Tefara, for the thousandth time, "and hidden the pearl and told no one, you would have it now."

"But Huru-Huru was with me when I opened the shell—have I not told you so times and times and times without end?"

"And now we shall have no house. Raoul told me to-day that if you had not sold the pearl to Toriki—"

"I did not sell it. Toriki robbed me."

"—that if you had not sold the pearl, he would give you five thousand French dollars, which is ten thousand Chili."

"He has been talking to his mother," Mapuhi explained. "She has an eye for a pearl."

"And now the pearl is lost," Tefara complained.

"It paid my debt with Toriki. That is twelve hundred I have made, anyway."

"Toriki is dead," she cried. "They have heard no word of his schooner. She was lost along with the *Aorai* and the *Hira*. Will Toriki pay you the three hundred credit he promised? No, because Toriki is dead. And had you found no pearl, would you to-day owe Toriki the twelve hundred? No, because Toriki is dead, and you cannot pay dead men."

"But Levy did not pay Toriki," Mapuhi said. "He gave him a piece of paper that was good for the money in Papeete; and now Levy is dead and cannot pay; and Toriki is dead and the paper lost with him, and the pearl is lost with Levy. You are right, Tefara. I have lost the pearl, and got nothing for it. Now let us sleep."

He held up his hand suddenly and listened. From without came a noise, as of one who breathed heavily and with pain. A hand fumbled against the mat that served for a door.

"Who is there?" Mapuhi cried.

"Nauri," came the answer. "Can you tell me where is my son, Mapuhi?"

Tefara screamed and gripped her husband's arm.

"A ghost!" she chattered. "A ghost!"

Mapuhi's face was a ghastly yellow. He clung weakly to his wife.

"Good woman," he said in faltering tones, striving to disguise his voice, "I know your son well. He is living on the east side of the lagoon."

From without came the sound of a sigh. Mapuhi began to feel elated. He had fooled the ghost.

"But where do you come from, old woman?" he asked.

"From the sea," was the dejected answer.

"I knew it! I knew it!" screamed Tefara, rocking to and fro.

"Since when has Tefara bedded in a strange house?" came Nauri's voice through the matting.

Mapuhi looked fear and reproach at his wife. It was her voice that had betrayed them.

"And since when has Mapuhi, my son, denied his old mother?" the voice went on.

"No, no, I have not—Mapuhi has not denied you," he cried. "I am not Mapuhi. He is on the east end of the lagoon, I tell you."

Ngakura sat up in bed and began to cry. The matting started to shake.

"What are you doing?" Mapuhi demanded.

"I am coming in," said the voice of Nauri.

One end of the matting lifted. Tefara tried to dive under the blankets, but Mapuhi held on to her. He had to hold on to something. Together, struggling with each other, with shivering bodies and chattering teeth, they gazed with protruding eyes at the lifting mat. They saw Nauri, dripping with sea-water, without her *ahu*, creep in. They rolled over backward from her and fought for Ngakura's blanket with which to cover their heads.

"You might give your old mother a drink of water," the ghost said plaintively.

"Give her a drink of water," Tefara commanded in a shaking voice.

"Give her a drink of water," Mapuhi passed on the command to Ngakura.

And together they kicked out Ngakura from under the blanket. A minute later, peeping, Mapuhi saw the ghost drinking. When it reached out a shaking hand and laid it on his, he felt the weight of it and was convinced that it was no ghost. Then he emerged, dragging Tefara after him, and in a few minutes all were listening to Nauri's tale. And when she told of Levy, and dropped the pearl into Tefara's hand, even she was reconciled to the reality of her mother-in-law.

"In the morning," said Tefara, "you will sell the pearl to Raoul for five thousand French."

"The house?" objected Nauri.

"He will build the house," Tefara answered. "He says it will cost four thousand French. Also will he give one thousand French in credit, which is two thousand Chili."

"And it will be six fathoms long?" Nauri queried.

"Ay," answered Mapuhi, "six fathoms."

"And in the middle room will be the octagon-drop-clock?"

"Ay, and the round table as well."

"Then give me something to eat, for I am hungry," said Nauri, complacently. "And after that we will sleep, for I am weary. And to-morrow we will have more talk about the house before we sell the pearl. It will be better if we take the thousand French in cash. Money is ever better than credit in buying goods from the traders."

The Whale Tooth

It was in the early days in Fiji, when John Starhurst arose in the mission-house at Rewa Village and announced his intention of carrying the Gospel throughout all Viti Levu. Now Viti Levu means the "Great Land," it being the largest island in a group composed of many large islands, to say nothing of hundreds of small ones. Here and there on the coasts, living by most precarious tenure, was a sprinkling of missionaries, traders, bêche-de-mer fishers, and whaleship deserters. The smoke of the hot ovens arose under their windows, and the bodies of the slain were dragged by their doors on the way to the feasting.

The Lotu, or the Worship, was progressing slowly, and, often, in crablike fashion. Chiefs, who announced themselves Christians and were welcomed into the body of the chapel, had a distressing habit of backsliding in order to partake of the flesh of some favorite enemy. Eat or be eaten had been the law of the land; and eat or be eaten promised to remain the law of the land for a long time to come. There were chiefs, such as Tanoa, Tuiveikoso, and Tuikilakila, who had literally eaten hundreds of their fellow-men. But among these gluttons Ra Undreundre ranked highest. Ra Undreundre lived at Takiraki. He kept a register of his gustatory exploits. A row of stones outside his house marked the bodies he had eaten. This row was two hundred and thirty paces long, and the stones in it numbered eight hundred and seventy-two. Each stone represented a body. The row of stones might have been longer, had not Ra Undreundre unfortunately received a spear in the small of his back in a bush skirmish on Somo Somo and been served up on the table of

Naungavuli, whose mediocre string of stones numbered only forty-eight.

The hard-worked, fever-stricken missionaries stuck doggedly to their task, at times despairing, and looking forward for some special manifestation, some outburst of Pentecostal fire that would bring a glorious harvest of souls. But cannibal Fiji had remained obdurate. The frizzle-headed man-eaters were loath to leave their flesh-pots so long as the harvest of human carcasses was plentiful. Sometimes, when the harvest was too plentiful, they imposed on the missionaries by letting the word slip out that on such a day there would be a killing and a barbecue. Promptly the missionaries would buy the lives of the victims with stick tobacco, fathoms of calico, and quarts of trade-beads. Natheless the chiefs drove a handsome trade in thus disposing of their surplus live meat. Also, they could always go out and catch more.

It was at this juncture that John Starhurst proclaimed that he would carry the Gospel from coast to coast of the Great Land, and that he would begin by penetrating the mountain fastnesses of the headwaters of the Rewa River. His words were received with consternation.

The native teachers wept softly. His two fellow-missionaries strove to dissuade him. The King of Rewa warned him that the mountain dwellers would surely kai-kai him—kai-kai meaning "to eat"—and that he, the King of Rewa, having become Lotu, would be put to the necessity of going to war with the mountain dwellers. That he could not conquer them he was perfectly aware. That they might come down the river and sack Rewa Village he was likewise perfectly aware. But what was he to do? If John Starhurst persisted in going out and being eaten, there would be a war that would cost hundreds of lives.

Later in the day a deputation of Rewa chiefs waited upon John Starhurst. He heard them patiently, and argued patiently with them, though he abated not a whit from his purpose. To his fellow-missionaries he explained that he was not bent upon martyrdom; that the call had come for him to carry the Gospel into Viti Levu, and that he was merely obeying the Lord's wish.

To the traders, who came and objected most strenuously of

all, he said: "Your objections are valueless. They consist merely of the damage that may be done your businesses. You are interested in making money, but I am interested in saving souls. The heathen of this dark land must be saved."

John Starhurst was not a fanatic. He would have been the first man to deny the imputation. He was eminently sane and practical. He was sure that his mission would result in good, and he had private visions of igniting the Pentecostal spark in the souls of the mountaineers and of inaugurating a revival that would sweep down out of the mountains and across the length and breadth of the Great Land from sea to sea and to the isles in the midst of the sea. There were no wild lights in his mild gray eyes, but only calm resolution and an unfaltering trust in the Higher Power that was guiding him.

One man only he found who approved of his project, and that was Ra Vatu, who secretly encouraged him and offered to lend him guides to the first foothills. John Starhurst, in turn, was greatly pleased by Ra Vatu's conduct. From an incorrigible heathen, with a heart as black as his practices, Ra Vatu was beginning to emanate light. He even spoke of becoming Lotu. True, three years before he had expressed a similar intention, and would have entered the church had not John Starhurst entered objection to his bringing his four wives along with him. Ra Vatu had had economic and ethical objections to monogamy. Besides, the missionary's hair-splitting objection had offended him; and, to prove that he was a free agent and a man of honor, he had swung his huge war-club over Starhurst's head. Starhurst had escaped by rushing in under the club and holding on to him until help arrived. But all that was now forgiven and forgotten. Ra Vatu was coming into the church, not merely as a converted heathen, but as a converted polygamist as well. He was only waiting, he assured Starhurst, until his oldest wife, who was very sick, should die.

John Starhurst journeyed up the sluggish Rewa in one of Ra Vatu's canoes. This canoe was to carry him for two days, when, the head of navigation reached, it would return. Far in the distance, lifted into the sky, could be seen the great smoky mountains that marked the backbone of the Great Land. All day John Starhurst gazed at them with eager yearning.

Sometimes he prayed silently. At other times he was joined in prayer by Narau, a native teacher, who for seven years had been Lotu, ever since the day he had been saved from the hot oven by Dr. James Ellery Brown at the trifling expense of one hundred sticks of tobacco, two cotton blankets, and a large bottle of painkiller. At the last moment, after twenty hours of solitary supplication and prayer, Narau's ears had heard the call to go forth with John Starhurst on the mission to the mountains.

"Master, I will surely go with thee," he had announced.

John Starhurst had hailed him with sober delight. Truly, the Lord was with him thus to spur on so broken-spirited a creature as Narau.

"I am indeed without spirit, the weakest of the Lord's vessels," Narau explained, the first day in the canoe.

"You should have faith, stronger faith," the missionary chided him.

Another canoe journeyed up the Rewa that day. But it journeyed an hour astern, and it took care not to be seen. This canoe was also the property of Ra Vatu. In it was Erirola, Ra Vatu's first cousin and trusted henchman; and in the small basket that never left his hand was a whale tooth. It was a magnificent tooth, fully six inches long, beautifully proportioned, the ivory turned yellow and purple with age. This tooth was likewise the property of Ra Vatu; and in Fiji, when such a tooth goes forth, things usually happen. For this is the virtue of the whale tooth: Whoever accepts it cannot refuse the request that may accompany it or follow it. The request may be anything from a human life to a tribal alliance, and no Fijian is so dead to honor as to deny the request when once the tooth has been accepted. Sometimes the request hangs fire, or the fulfilment is delayed, with untoward consequences.

High up the Rewa, at the village of a chief, Mongondro by name, John Starhurst rested at the end of the second day of the journey. In the morning, attended by Narau, he expected to start on foot for the smoky mountains that were now green and velvety with nearness. Mongondro was a sweet-tempered, mild-mannered little old chief, short-sighted and afflicted with elephantiasis, and no longer inclined toward the turbulence of war.

He received the missionary with warm hospitality, gave him food from his own table, and even discussed religious matters with him. Mongondro was of an inquiring bent of mind, and pleased John Starhurst greatly by asking him to account for the existence and beginning of things. When the missionary had finished his summary of the Creation according to Genesis, he saw that Mongondro was deeply affected. The little old chief smoked silently for some time. Then he took the pipe from his mouth and shook his head sadly.

"It cannot be," he said. "I, Mongondro, in my youth, was a good workman with the adze. Yet three months did it take me to make a canoe—a small canoe, a very small canoe. And you say that all this land and water was made by one man—"

"Nay, was made by one God, the only true God," the missionary interrupted.

"It is the same thing," Mongondro went on, "that all the land and all the water, the trees, the fish, and bush and mountains, the sun, the moon, and the stars, were made in six days! No, no. I tell you that in my youth I was an able man, yet did it require me three months for one small canoe. It is a story to frighten children with; but no man can believe it."

"I am a man," the missionary said.

"True, you are a man. But it is not given to my dark understanding to know what you believe."

"I tell you, I do believe that everything was made in six days."

"So you say, so you say," the old cannibal murmured soothingly.

It was not until after John Starhurst and Narau had gone off to bed that Erirola crept into the chief's house, and, after diplomatic speech, handed the whale tooth to Mongondro.

The old chief held the tooth in his hands for a long time. It was a beautiful tooth, and he yearned for it. Also, he divined the request that must accompany it. "No, no; whale teeth were beautiful," and his mouth watered for it, but he passed it back to Erirola with many apologies.

⬥   ⬥   ⬥   ⬥   ⬥   ⬥

In the early dawn John Starhurst was afoot, striding along the bush trail in his big leather boots, at his heels the faithful Narau, himself at the heels of a naked guide lent him by Mongondro to show the way to the next village, which was reached by midday. Here a new guide showed the way. A mile in the rear plodded Erirola, the whale tooth in the basket slung on his shoulder. For two days more he brought up the missionary's rear, offering the tooth to the village chiefs. But village after village refused the tooth. It followed so quickly the missionary's advent that they divined the request that would be made, and would have none of it.

They were getting deep into the mountains, and Erirola took a secret trail, cut in ahead of the missionary, and reached the stronghold of the Buli of Gatoka. Now the Buli was unaware of John Starhurst's imminent arrival. Also, the tooth was beautiful—an extraordinary specimen, while the coloring of it was of the rarest order. The tooth was presented publicly. The Buli of Gatoka, seated on his best mat, surrounded by his chief men, three busy fly-brushers at his back, deigned to receive from the hand of his herald the whale tooth presented by Ra Vatu and carried into the mountains by his cousin, Erirola. A clapping of hands went up at the acceptation of the present, the assembled headmen, heralds, and fly-brushers crying aloud in chorus:

"A! woi! woi! woi! A! woi! woi! woi! A tabua levu! woi! woi! A mudua, mudua, mudua!"

"Soon will come a man, a white man," Erirola began, after the proper pause. "He is a missionary man, and he will come to-day. Ra Vatu is pleased to desire his boots. He wishes to present them to his good friend, Mongondro, and it is in his mind to send them with the feet along in them, for Mongondro is an old man and his teeth are not good. Be sure, O Buli, that the feet go along in the boots. As for the rest of him, it may stop here."

The delight in the whale tooth faded out of the Buli's eyes, and he glanced about him dubiously. Yet had he already accepted the tooth.

"A little thing like a missionary does not matter," Erirola prompted.

"No, a little thing like a missionary does not matter," the Buli answered, himself again. "Mongondro shall have the boots. Go, you young men, some three or four of you, and meet the missionary on the trail. Be sure you bring back the boots as well."

"It is too late," said Erirola. "Listen! He comes now."

Breaking through the thicket of brush, John Starhurst, with Narau close on his heels, strode upon the scene. The famous boots, having filled in wading the stream, squirted fine jets of water at every step. Starhurst looked about him with flashing eyes. Upborne by an unwavering trust, untouched by doubt or fear, he exulted in all he saw. He knew that since the beginning of time he was the first white man ever to tread the mountain stronghold of Gatoka.

The grass houses clung to the steep mountain side or overhung the rushing Rewa. On either side towered a mighty precipice. At the best, three hours of sunlight penetrated that narrow gorge. No cocoanuts nor bananas were to be seen, though dense, tropic vegetation overran everything, dripping in airy festoons from the sheer lips of the precipices and running riot in all the crannied ledges. At the far end of the gorge the Rewa leaped eight hundred feet in a single span, while the atmosphere of the rock fortress pulsed to the rhythmic thunder of the fall.

From the Buli's house John Starhurst saw emerging the Buli and his followers.

"I bring you good tidings," was the missionary's greeting.

"Who has sent you?" the Buli rejoined quietly.

"God."

"It is a new name in Viti Levu," the Buli grinned. "Of what islands, villages, or passes may he be chief?"

"He is the chief over all islands, all villages, all passes," John Starhurst answered solemnly. "He is the Lord over heaven and earth, and I am come to bring His word to you."

"Has he sent whale teeth?" was the insolent query.

"No, but more precious than whale teeth is the—"

"It is the custom, between chiefs, to send whale teeth," the Buli interrupted. "Your chief is either a niggard, or you are a fool, to come empty-handed into the mountains. Behold, a more generous than you is before you."

So saying, he showed the whale tooth he had received from Erirola.

Narau groaned.

"It is the whale tooth of Ra Vatu," he whispered to Starhurst.
"I know it well. Now are we undone."

"A gracious thing," the missionary answered, passing his hand
through his long beard and adjusting his glasses. "Ra Vatu has
arranged that we should be well received."

But Narau groaned again, and backed away from the heels he
had dogged so faithfully.

"Ra Vatu is soon to become Lotu," Starhurst explained, "and
I have come bringing the Lotu to you."

"I want none of your Lotu," said the Buli, proudly. "And it is
in my mind that you will be clubbed this day."

The Buli nodded to one of his big mountaineers, who stepped
forward, swinging a club. Narau bolted into the nearest house,
seeking to hide among the women and mats; but John Starhurst
sprang in under the club and threw his arms around his execu-
tioner's neck. From this point of vantage he proceeded to argue.
He was arguing for his life, and he knew it; but he was neither
excited nor afraid.

"It would be an evil thing for you to kill me," he told the man.
"I have done you no wrong, nor have I done the Buli wrong."

So well did he cling to the neck of the one man that they
dared not strike with their clubs. And he continued to cling
and to dispute for his life with those who clamored for his
death.

"I am John Starhurst," he went on calmly. "I have labored in
Fiji for three years, and I have done it for no profit. I am here
among you for good. Why should any man kill me? To kill me
will not profit any man."

The Buli stole a look at the whale tooth. He was well paid for
the deed.

The missionary was surrounded by a mass of naked savages,
all struggling to get at him. The death song, which is the song of
the oven, was raised, and his expostulations could no longer be
heard. But so cunningly did he twine and wreathe his body
about his captor's that the deathblow could not be struck.
Erirola smiled, and the Buli grew angry.

"Away with you!" he cried. "A nice story to go back to the

coast—a dozen of you and one missionary, without weapons, weak as a woman, overcoming all of you."

"Wait, O Buli," John Starhurst called out from the thick of the scuffle, "and I will overcome even you. For my weapons are Truth and Right, and no man can withstand them."

"Come to me, then," the Buli answered, "for my weapon is only a poor miserable club, and, as you say, it cannot withstand you."

The group separated from him, and John Starhurst stood alone, facing the Buli, who was leaning on an enormous, knotted warclub.

"Come to me, missionary man, and overcome me," the Buli challenged.

"Even so will I come to you and overcome you," John Starhurst made answer, first wiping his spectacles and settling them properly, then beginning his advance.

The Buli raised the club and waited.

"In the first place, my death will profit you nothing," began the argument.

"I leave the answer to my club," was the Buli's reply.

And to every point he made the same reply, at the same time watching the missionary closely in order to forestall that cunning run-in under the lifted club. Then, and for the first time, John Starhurst knew that his death was at hand. He made no attempt to run in. Bareheaded, he stood in the sun and prayed aloud—the mysterious figure of the inevitable white man, who, with Bible, bullet, or rum bottle, has confronted the amazed savage in his every stronghold. Even so stood John Starhurst in the rock fortress of the Buli of Gatoka.

"Forgive them, for they know not what they do," he prayed. "O Lord! have mercy upon Fiji. Have compassion for Fiji. O Jehovah, hear us for His sake, Thy Son, whom Thou didst give that through Him all men might also become Thy children. From Thee we came, and our mind is that to Thee we may return. The land is dark, O Lord, the land is dark. But Thou art mighty to save. Reach out Thy hand, O Lord, and save Fiji, poor cannibal Fiji."

The Buli grew impatient.

"Now will I answer thee," he muttered, at the same time swinging his club with both hands.

Narau, hiding among the women and the mats, heard the impact of the blow and shuddered. Then the death song arose, and he knew his beloved missionary's body was being dragged to the oven as he heard the words:

"Drag me gently. Drag me gently."

"For I am the champion of my land."

"Give thanks! Give thanks! Give thanks!"

Next, a single voice arose out of the din, asking:

"Where is the brave man?"

A hundred voices bellowed the answer:

"Gone to be dragged into the oven and cooked."

"Where is the coward?" the single voice demanded.

"Gone to report!" the hundred voices bellowed back. "Gone to report! Gone to report!"

Narau groaned in anguish of spirit. The words of the old song were true. He was the coward, and nothing remained to him but to go and report.

Mauki

He weighed one hundred and ten pounds. His hair was kinky and negroid, and he was black. He was peculiarly black. He was neither blue-black nor purple-black, but plum-black. His name was Mauki, and he was the son of a chief. He had three *tambos*. *Tambo* is Melanesian for *taboo*, and is first cousin to that Polynesian word. Mauki's three *tambos* were as follows: first, he must never shake hands with a woman, nor have a woman's hand touch him or any of his personal belongings; secondly, he must never eat clams nor any food from a fire in which clams had been cooked; thirdly, he must never touch a crocodile, nor travel in a canoe that carried any part of a crocodile even if as large as a tooth.

Of a different black were his teeth, which were deep black, or, perhaps better, *lamp*-black. They had been made so in a single night, by his mother, who had compressed about them a powdered mineral which was dug from the landslide back of Port Adams. Port Adams is a saltwater village on Malaita, and Malaita is the most savage island in the Solomons—so savage that no traders nor planters have yet gained a foothold on it; while, from the time of the earliest bêche-de-mer fishers and sandalwood traders down to the latest labor recruiters equipped with automatic rifles and gasolene engines, scores of white adventurers have been passed out by tomahawks and soft-nosed Snider bullets. So Malaita remains to-day, in the twentieth century, the stamping ground of the labor recruiters, who farm its coasts for laborers who engage and contract themselves to toil on the plantations of the neighboring and more civilized islands

34

for a wage of thirty dollars a year. The natives of those neighboring and more civilized islands have themselves become too
civilized to work on plantations.

Mauki's ears were pierced, not in one place, nor two places,
but in a couple of dozen places. In one of the smaller holes he
carried a clay pipe. The larger holes were too large for such use.
The bowl of the pipe would have fallen through. In fact, in the
largest hole in each ear he habitually wore round wooden plugs
that were an even four inches in diameter. Roughly speaking,
the circumference of said holes was twelve and one-half inches.
Mauki was catholic in his tastes. In the various smaller holes he
carried such things as empty rifle cartridges, horseshoe nails,
copper screws, pieces of string, braids of sennit, strips of green
leaf, and, in the cool of the day, scarlet hibiscus flowers. From
which it will be seen that pockets were not necessary to his well-
being. Besides, pockets were impossible, for his only wearing
apparel consisted of a piece of calico several inches wide. A
pocket knife he wore in his hair, the blade snapped down on a
kinky lock. His most prized possession was the handle of a china
cup, which he suspended from a ring of turtle-shell, which, in
turn, was passed through the partition-cartilage of his nose.

But in spite of embellishments, Mauki had a nice face. It was
really a pretty face, viewed by any standard, and for a
Melanesian it was a remarkably good-looking face. Its one fault
was its lack of strength. It was softly effeminate, almost girlish.
The features were small, regular, and delicate. The chin was
weak, and the mouth was weak. There was no strength nor char-
acter in the jaws, forehead, and nose. In the eyes only could be
caught any hint of the unknown quantities that were so large a
part of his make-up and that other persons could not understand. These unknown quantities were pluck, pertinacity, fear-
lessness, imagination, and cunning; and when they found
expression in some consistent and striking action, those about
him were astounded.

Mauki's father was chief over the village at Port Adams, and
thus, by birth a saltwater man, Mauki was half amphibian. He
knew the way of the fishes and oysters, and the reef was an open
book to him. Canoes, also, he knew. He learned to swim when

he was a year old. At seven years he could hold his breath a full minute and swim straight down to bottom through thirty feet of water. And at seven years he was stolen by the bushmen, who cannot even swim and who are afraid of salt water. Thereafter Mauki saw the sea only from a distance, through rifts in the jungle and from open spaces on the high mountain sides. He became the slave of old Fanfoa, head chief over a score of scattered bush-villages on the range-lips of Malaita, the smoke of which, on calm mornings, is about the only evidence the seafaring white men have of the teeming interior population. For the whites do not penetrate Malaita. They tried it once, in the days when the search was on for gold, but they always left their heads behind to grin from the smoky rafters of the bushmen's huts.

When Mauki was a young man of seventeen, Fanfoa got out of tobacco. He got dreadfully out of tobacco. It was hard times in all his villages. He had been guilty of a mistake. Suo was a harbor so small that a large schooner could not swing at anchor in it. It was surrounded by mangroves that overhung the deep water. It was a trap, and into the trap sailed two white men in a small ketch. They were after recruits, and they possessed much tobacco and trade-goods, to say nothing of three rifles and plenty of ammunition. Now there were no saltwater men living at Suo, and it was there that the bushmen could come down to the sea. The ketch did a splendid traffic. It signed on twenty recruits the first day. Even old Fanfoa signed on. And that same day the score of new recruits chopped off the two white men's heads, killed the boat's crew, and burned the ketch. Thereafter, and for three months, there was tobacco and trade-goods in plenty and to spare in all the bush-villages. Then came the man-of-war that threw shells for miles into the hills, frightening the people out of their villages and into the deeper bush. Next the man-of-war sent landing parties ashore. The villages were all burned, along with the tobacco and trade-stuff. The cocoanuts and bananas were chopped down, the taro gardens uprooted, and the pigs and chickens killed.

It taught Fanfoa a lesson, but in the meantime he was out of tobacco. Also, his young men were too frightened to sign on with the recruiting vessels. That was why Fanfoa ordered his slave, Mauki, to be carried down and signed on for half a case of tobacco advance, along with knives, axes, calico, and beads, which he would pay for with his toil on the plantations. Mauki was sorely frightened when they brought him on board the schooner. He was a lamb led to the slaughter. White men were ferocious creatures. They had to be, or else they would not make a practice of venturing along the Malaita coast and into all harbors, two on a schooner, when each schooner carried from fifteen to twenty blacks as boat's crew, and often as high as sixty or seventy black recruits. In addition to this, there was always the danger of the shore population, the sudden attack and the cutting off of the schooner and all hands. Truly, white men must be terrible. Besides, they were possessed of such devil-devils— rifles that shot very rapidly many times, things of iron and brass that made the schooners go when there was no wind, and boxes that talked and laughed just as men talked and laughed. Ay, and he had heard of one white man whose particular devil-devil was so powerful that he could take out all his teeth and put them back at will.

Down into the cabin they took Mauki. On deck, the one white man kept guard with two revolvers in his belt. In the cabin the other white man sat with a book before him, in which he inscribed strange marks and lines. He looked at Mauki as though he had been a pig or a fowl, glanced under the hollows of his arms, and wrote in the book. Then he held out the writing stick and Mauki just barely touched it with his hand, in so doing pledging himself to toil for three years on the plantations of the Moongleam Soap Company. It was not explained to him that the will of the ferocious white men would be used to enforce the pledge, and that, behind all, for the same use, was all the power and all the warships of Great Britain.

Other blacks there were on board, from unheard-of far places, and when the white man spoke to them, they tore the long feather from Mauki's hair, cut that same hair short, and wrapped about his waist a lava-lava of bright yellow calico.

After many days on the schooner, and after beholding more land and islands than he had ever dreamed of, he was landed on New Georgia, and put to work in the field clearing jungle and cutting cane grass. For the first time he knew what work was. Even as a slave to Fanfoa he had not worked like this. And he did not like work. It was up at dawn and in at dark, on two meals a day. And the food was tiresome. For weeks at a time they were given nothing but sweet potatoes to eat, and for weeks at a time it would be nothing but rice. He cut out the cocoanut from the shells day after day; and for long days and weeks he fed the fires that smoked the copra, till his eyes got sore and he was set to felling trees. He was a good axe-man, and later he was put in the bridge-building gang. Once, he was punished by being put in the road-building gang. At times he served as boat's crew in the whale-boats, when they brought in copra from distant beaches or when the white men went out to dynamite fish.

Among other things he learned bêche-de-mer English, with which he could talk with all white men, and with all recruits who otherwise would have talked in a thousand different dialects. Also, he learned certain things about the white men, principally that they kept their word. If they told a boy he was going to receive a stick of tobacco, he got it. If they told a boy they would knock seven bells out of him if he did a certain thing, when he did that thing seven bells invariably were knocked out of him. Mauki did not know what seven bells were, but they occurred in bêche-de-mer, and he imagined them to be the blood and teeth that sometimes accompanied the process of knocking out seven bells. One other thing he learned: no boy was struck or punished unless he did wrong. Even when the white men were drunk, as they were frequently, they never struck unless a rule had been broken.

Mauki did not like the plantation. He hated work, and he was the son of a chief. Furthermore, it was ten years since he had been stolen from Port Adams by Fanfoa, and he was homesick. He was even homesick for the slavery under Fanfoa. So he ran away. He struck back into the bush, with the idea of working southward to the beach and stealing a canoe in which to go home to Port Adams. But the fever got him, and he was captured and brought back more dead than alive.

A second time he ran away, in the company of two Malaita boys. They got down the coast twenty miles, and were hidden in the hut of a Malaita freeman, who dwelt in that village. But in the dead of night two white men came, who were not afraid of all the village people and who knocked seven bells out of the three runaways, tied them like pigs, and tossed them into the whale-boat. But the man in whose house they had hidden— seven times seven bells must have been knocked out of him from the way the hair, skin, and teeth flew, and he was discouraged for the rest of his natural life from harboring runaway laborers.

For a year Mauki toiled on. Then he was made a house-boy, and had good food and easy times, with light work in keeping the house clean and serving the white men with whiskey and beer at all hours of the day and most hours of the night. He liked it, but he liked Port Adams more. He had two years longer to serve, but two years were too long for him in the throes of homesickness. He had grown wiser with his year of service, and, being now a house-boy, he had opportunity. He had the cleaning of the rifles, and he knew where the key to the store-room was hung. He planned the escape, and one night ten Malaita boys and one boy from San Cristoval sneaked from the barracks and dragged one of the whale-boats down to the beach. It was Mauki who supplied the key that opened the padlock on the boat, and it was Mauki who equipped the boat with a dozen Winchesters, an immense amount of ammunition, a case of dynamite with detonators and fuse, and ten cases of tobacco.

The northwest monsoon was blowing, and they fled south in the night-time, hiding by day on detached and uninhabited islets, or dragging their whale-boat into the bush on the large islands. Thus they gained Guadalcanar, skirted halfway along it, and crossed the Indispensable Straits to Florida Island. It was here that they killed the San Cristoval boy, saving his head and cooking and eating the rest of him. The Malaita coast was only twenty miles away, but the last night a strong current and baffling winds prevented them from gaining across. Daylight found them still several miles from their goal. But daylight brought a cutter, in which were two white men, who were not afraid of eleven Malaita men armed with twelve rifles. Mauki and his companions were carried back to Tulagi, where lived the great white master of all the white men. And the great white master held a court, after which, one by one, the runaways were tied up and given twenty lashes each, and sentenced to a fine of fifteen dollars. Then they were sent back to New Georgia, where the white men knocked seven bells out of them all around and put them to work. But Mauki was no longer house-boy. He was put in the road-making gang. The fine of fifteen dollars had been paid by the white men from whom he had run away, and he was told that he would have to work it out, which meant six months' additional toil. Further, his share of the stolen tobacco earned him another year of toil.

Port Adams was now three years and a half away, so he stole a canoe one night, hid on the islets in Manning Straits, passed through the Straits, and began working along the eastern coast of Ysabel, only to be captured, two-thirds of the way along, by the white men on Meringe Lagoon. After a week, he escaped from them and took to the bush. There were no bush natives on Ysabel, only saltwater men, who were all Christians. The white men put up a reward of five hundred sticks of tobacco, and every time Mauki ventured down to the sea to steal a canoe he was chased by the saltwater men. Four months of this passed, when, the reward having been raised to a thousand sticks, he was caught and sent back to New Georgia and the road-building gang. Now a thousand sticks are worth fifty dollars, and Mauki had to pay the reward himself, which required a year and eight months' labor. So Port Adams was now five years away.

His homesickness was greater than ever, and it did not appeal to him to settle down and be good, work out his four years, and go home. The next time, he was caught in the very act of running away. His case was brought before Mr. Haveby, the island manager of the Moongleam Soap Company, who adjudged him an incorrigible. The Company had plantations on the Santa Cruz Islands, hundreds of miles across the sea, and there it sent its Solomon Islands' incorrigibles. And there Mauki was sent, though he never arrived. The schooner stopped at Santa Anna, and in the night Mauki swam ashore, where he stole two rifles and a case of tobacco from the trader and got away in a canoe to Cristoval. Malaita was now to the north, fifty or sixty miles away. But when he attempted the passage, he was caught by a light gale and driven back to Santa Anna, where the trader clapped him in irons and held him against the return of the schooner from Santa Cruz. The two rifles the trader recovered, but the case of tobacco was charged up to Mauki at the rate of another year. The sum of years he now owed the Company was six.

On the way back to New Georgia, the schooner dropped anchor in Marau Sound, which lies at the southeastern extremity of Guadalcanar. Mauki swam ashore with handcuffs on his wrists and got away to the bush. The schooner went on, but the Moongleam trader ashore offered a thousand sticks, and to him Mauki was brought by the bushmen with a year and eight months tacked on to his account. Again, and before the schooner called in, he got away, this time in a whale-boat accompanied by a case of the trader's tobacco. But a northwest gale wrecked him upon Ugi, where the Christian natives stole his tobacco and turned him over to the Moongleam trader who resided there. The tobacco the natives stole meant another year for him, and the tale was now eight years and a half.

"We'll send him to Lord Howe," said Mr. Haveby. "Bunster is there, and we'll let them settle it between them. It will be a case, I imagine, of Mauki getting Bunster, or Bunster getting Mauki, and good riddance in either event."

If one leaves Meringe Lagoon, on Ysabel, and steers a course due north, magnetic, at the end of one hundred and fifty miles he will lift the pounded coral beaches of Lord Howe above the sea. Lord Howe is a ring of land some one hundred and fifty miles in circumference, several hundred yards wide at its widest, and towering in places to a height of ten feet above sea-level. Inside this ring of sand is a mighty lagoon studded with coral patches. Lord Howe belongs to the Solomons neither geographically nor ethnologically. It is an atoll, while the Solomons are high islands; and its people and language are Polynesian, while the inhabitants of the Solomons are Melanesian. Lord Howe has been populated by the westward Polynesian drift which continues to this day, big outrigger canoes being washed upon its beaches by the southeast trade. That there has been a slight Melanesian drift in the period of the northwest monsoon, is also evident.

Nobody ever comes to Lord Howe, or Ontong-Java as it is sometimes called. Thomas Cook & Son do not sell tickets to it, and tourists do not dream of its existence. Not even a white missionary has landed on its shore. Its five thousand natives are as peaceable as they are primitive. Yet they were not always peaceable. The *Sailing Directions* speak of them as hostile and treacherous. But the men who compile the *Sailing Directions* have never heard of the change that was worked in the hearts of the inhabitants, who, not many years ago, cut off a big bark and killed all hands with the exception of the second mate. This survivor carried the news to his brothers. The captains of three trading schooners returned with him to Lord Howe. They sailed their vessels right into the lagoon and proceeded to preach the white man's gospel that only white men shall kill white men and that the lesser breeds must keep hands off. The schooners sailed up and down the lagoon, harrying and destroying. There was no escape from the narrow sand-circle, no bush to which to flee. The men were shot down at sight, and there was no avoiding being sighted. The villages were burned, the canoes smashed, the chickens and pigs killed, and the precious cocoanut-trees chopped down. For a month this continued, when the schooners sailed away; but the fear of the white man had been seared into the souls of the islanders and never again were they rash enough to harm one.

Max Bunster was the one white man on Lord Howe, trading in the pay of the ubiquitous Moongleam Soap Company. And the Company billeted him on Lord Howe, because, next to getting rid of him, it was the most out-of-the-way place to be found. That the Company did not get rid of him was due to the difficulty of finding another man to take his place. He was a strapping big German, with something wrong in his brain. Semi-madness would be a charitable statement of his condition. He was a bully and a coward, and a thrice-bigger savage than any savage on the island. Being a coward, his brutality was of the cowardly order. When he first went into the Company's employ, he was stationed on Savo. When a consumptive colonial was sent to take his place, he beat him up with his fists and sent him off a wreck in the schooner that brought him.

Mr. Haveby next selected a young Yorkshire giant to relieve Bunster. The Yorkshire man had a reputation as a bruiser and preferred fighting to eating. But Bunster wouldn't fight. He was a regular little lamb—for ten days, at the end of which time the Yorkshire man was prostrated by a combined attack of dysentery and fever. Then Bunster went for him, among other things getting him down and jumping on him a score or so of times. Afraid of what would happen when his victim recovered, Bunster fled away in a cutter to Guvutu, where he signalized himself by beating up a young Englishman already crippled by a Boer bullet through both hips.

Then it was that Mr. Haveby sent Bunster to Lord Howe, the falling-off place. He celebrated his landing by mopping up half a case of gin and by thrashing the elderly and wheezy mate of the schooner which had brought him. When the schooner departed, he called the kanakas down to the beach and challenged them to throw him in a wrestling bout, promising a case of tobacco to the one who succeeded. Three kanakas he threw, but was promptly thrown by a fourth, who, instead of receiving the tobacco, got a bullet through his lungs.

And so began Bunster's reign on Lord Howe. Three thousand people lived in the principal village; but it was deserted, even in broad day, when he passed through. Men, women, and children fled before him. Even the dogs and pigs got out of the way, while the king was not above hiding under a mat. The two prime ministers lived in terror of Bunster, who never discussed any moot subject, but struck out with his fists instead.

And to Lord Howe came Mauki, to toil for Bunster for eight long years and a half. There was no escaping from Lord Howe. For better or worse, Bunster and he were tied together. Bunster weighed two hundred pounds. Mauki weighed one hundred and ten. Bunster was a degenerate brute. But Mauki was a primitive savage. While both had wills and ways of their own.

Mauki had no idea of the sort of master he was to work for. He had had no warnings, and he had concluded as a matter of course that Bunster would be like other white men, a drinker of

much whiskey, a ruler and a lawgiver who always kept his word
and who never struck a boy undeserved. Bunster had the advantage. He knew all about Mauki, and gloated over the coming
into possession of him. The last cook was suffering from a broken arm and a dislocated shoulder, so Bunster made Mauki cook
and general house-boy.

And Mauki soon learned that there were white men and
white men. On the very day the schooner departed he was
ordered to buy a chicken from Samisee, the native Tongan missionary. But Samisee had sailed across the lagoon and would not
be back for three days. Mauki returned with the information.
He climbed the steep stairway (the house stood on piles twelve
feet above the sand), and entered the living-room to report. The
trader demanded the chicken. Mauki opened his mouth to
explain the missionary's absence. But Bunster did not care for
explanations. He struck out with his fist. The blow caught Mauki
on the mouth and lifted him into the air. Clear through the
doorway he flew, across the narrow veranda, breaking the top
railing, and down to the ground. His lips were a contused,
shapeless mass, and his mouth was full of blood and broken
teeth.

"That'll teach you that back talk don't go with me," the trader
shouted, purple with rage, peering down at him over the broken
railing.

Mauki had never met a white man like this, and he resolved
to walk small and never offend. He saw the boat-boys knocked
about, and one of them put in irons for three days with nothing
to eat for the crime of breaking a rowlock while pulling. Then,
too, he heard the gossip of the village and learned why Bunster
had taken a third wife—by force, as was well known. The first
and second wives lay in the graveyard, under the white coral
sand, with slabs of coral rock at head and feet. They had died, it
was said, from beatings he had given them. The third wife was
certainly ill-used, as Mauki could see for himself.

But there was no way by which to avoid offending the white
man, who seemed offended with life. When Mauki kept silent,
he was struck and called a sullen brute. When he spoke, he was
struck for giving back talk. When he was grave, Bunster accused

him of plotting and gave him a thrashing in advance; and when he strove to be cheerful and to smile, he was charged with sneering at his lord and master and given a taste of stick. Bunster was a devil. The village would have done for him, had it not remembered the lesson of the three schooners. It might have done for him anyway, if there had been a bush to which to flee. As it was, the murder of the white men, of any white man, would bring a man-of-war that would kill the offenders and chop down the precious cocoanut-trees. Then there were the boat-boys, with minds fully made up to drown him by accident at the first opportunity to capsize the cutter. Only Bunster saw to it that the boat did not capsize.

Mauki was of a different breed, and, escape being impossible while Bunster lived, he was resolved to get the white man. The trouble was that he could never find a chance. Bunster was always on guard. Day and night his revolvers were ready to hand. He permitted nobody to pass behind his back, as Mauki learned after having been knocked down several times. Bunster knew that he had more to fear from the good-natured, even sweet-faced, Malaita boy than from the entire population of Lord Howe; and it gave added zest to the programme of torment he was carrying out. And Mauki walked small, accepted his punishments, and waited.

All other white men had respected his *tambos,* but not so Bunster. Mauki's weekly allowance of tobacco was two sticks. Bunster passed them to his woman and ordered Mauki to receive them from her hand. But this could not be, and Mauki went without his tobacco. In the same way he was made to miss many a meal, and to go hungry many a day. He was ordered to make chowder out of the big clams that grew in the lagoon. This he could not do, for clams were *tambo.* Six times in succession he refused to touch the clams, and six times he was knocked senseless. Bunster knew that the boy would die first, but called his refusal mutiny, and would have killed him had there been another cook to take his place.

One of the trader's favorite tricks was to catch Mauki's kinky locks and bat his head against the wall. Another trick was to catch Mauki unawares and thrust the live end of a cigar against his flesh. This Bunster called vaccination, and Mauki was vaccinated a number of times a week. Once, in a rage, Bunster ripped the cup handle from Mauki's nose, tearing the hole clear out of the cartilage.

"Oh, what a mug!" was his comment, when he surveyed the damage he had wrought.

The skin of a shark is like sandpaper, but the skin of a ray fish is like a rasp. In the South Seas the natives use it ás a wood file in smoothing down canoes and paddles. Bunster had a mitten made of ray fish skin. The first time he tried it on Mauki, with one sweep of the hand it fetched the skin off his back from neck to armpit. Bunster was delighted. He gave his wife a taste of the mitten, and tried it out thoroughly on the boat-boys. The prime ministers came in for a stroke each, and they had to grin and take it for a joke.

"Laugh, damn you, laugh!" was the cue he gave.

Mauki came in for the largest share of the mitten. Never a day passed without a caress from it. There were times when the loss of so much cuticle kept him awake at night, and often the half-healed surface was raked raw afresh by the facetious Mr. Bunster. Mauki continued his patient wait, secure in the knowledge that sooner or later his time would come. And he knew just what he was going to do, down to the smallest detail, when the time did come.

One morning Bunster got up in a mood for knocking seven bells out of the universe. He began on Mauki, and wound up on Mauki, in the interval knocking down his wife and hammering all the boat-boys. At breakfast he called the coffee slops and threw the scalding contents of the cup into Mauki's face. By ten o'clock Bunster was shivering with ague, and half an hour later he was burning with fever. It was no ordinary attack. It quickly became pernicious, and developed into black-water fever. The days passed, and he grew weaker and weaker, never leaving his bed. Mauki waited and watched, the while his skin grew intact once more. He ordered the boys to beach the cutter, scrub her bottom, and give her a general overhauling. They thought the order emanated from Bunster, and they obeyed. But Bunster at the time was lying unconscious and giving no orders. This was Mauki's chance, but still he waited.

When the worst was past, and Bunster lay convalescent and conscious, but weak as a baby, Mauki packed his few trinkets, including the china cup handle, into his trade box. Then he went over to the village and interviewed the king and his two prime ministers.

"This fella Bunster, him good fella you like too much?" he asked.

They explained in one voice that they liked the trader not at all. The ministers poured forth a recital of all the indignities and wrongs that had been heaped upon them. The king broke down and wept. Mauki interrupted rudely.

"You savve me—me big fella marster my country. You no like 'm this fella white marster. Me no like 'm. Plenty good you put hundred cocoanut, two hundred cocoanut, three hundred cocoanut along cutter. Him finish, you go sleep 'm good fella. Altogether kanaka sleep 'm good fella. Bime by big fella noise along house, you no savve hear 'm that fella noise. You altogether sleep strong fella too much."

In like manner Mauki interviewed the boat-boys. Then he ordered Bunster's wife to return to her family house. Had she refused, he would have been in a quandary, for his *tambo* would not have permitted him to lay hands on her.

The house deserted, he entered the sleeping-room, where the trader lay in a doze. Mauki first removed the revolvers, then placed the ray fish mitten on his hand. Bunster's first warning was a stroke of the mitten that removed the skin the full length of his nose.

"Good fella, eh?" Mauki grinned, between two strokes, one of which swept the forehead bare and the other of which cleaned off one side of his face. "Laugh, damn you, laugh."

Mauki did his work thoroughly, and the kanakas, hiding in their houses, heard the "big fella noise" that Bunster made and continued to make for an hour or more.

When Mauki was done, he carried the boat compass and all the rifles and ammunition down to the cutter, which he proceeded to ballast with cases of tobacco. It was while engaged in this that a hideous, skinless thing came out of the house and ran screaming down the beach till it fell in the sand and mewed and gibbered under the scorching sun. Mauki looked toward it and hesitated. Then he went over and removed the head, which he wrapped in a mat and stowed in the stern-locker of the cutter.

So soundly did the kanakas sleep through that long hot day that they did not see the cutter run out through the passage and head south, close-hauled on the southeast trade. Nor was the cutter ever sighted on that long tack to the shores of Ysabel, and during the tedious head-beat from there to Malaita. He landed at Port Adams with a wealth of rifles and tobacco such as no one man had ever possessed before. But he did not stop there. He had taken a white man's head, and only the bush could shelter him. So back he went to the bush-villages, where he shot old Fanfoa and half a dozen of the chief men, and made himself the chief over all the villages. When his father died, Mauki's brother ruled in Port Adams, and, joined together, saltwater men and bushmen, the resulting combination was the strongest of the ten score fighting tribes of Malaita.

More than his fear of the British government was Mauki's fear of the all-powerful Moongleam Soap Company; and one day a message came up to him in the bush, reminding him that he owed the Company eight and one-half years of labor. He sent back a favorable answer, and then appeared the inevitable white man, the captain of the schooner, the only white man during Mauki's reign who ventured the bush and came out alive. This man not only came out, but he brought with him seven hundred and fifty dollars in gold sovereigns—the money price of eight years and a half of labor plus the cost price of certain rifles and cases of tobacco.

Mauki no longer weighs one hundred and ten pounds. His stomach is three times its former girth, and he has four wives. He has many other things—rifles and revolvers, the handle of a china cup, and an excellent collection of bushmen's heads. But more precious than the entire collection is another head, perfectly dried and cured, with sandy hair and a yellowish beard, which is kept wrapped in the finest of fibre lava-lavas. When Mauki goes to war with villages beyond his realm, he invariably gets out this head, and, alone in his grass palace, contemplates it long and solemnly. At such times the hush of death falls on the village, and not even a pickaninny dares make a noise. The head is esteemed the most powerful devil-devil on Malaita, and to the possession of it is ascribed all of Mauki's greatness.

"Yah! Yah! Yah!"

He was a whiskey-guzzling Scotchman, and he downed his whiskey neat, beginning with his first tot punctually at six in the morning, and thereafter repeating it at regular intervals throughout the day till bed-time, which was usually midnight. He slept but five hours out of twenty-four, and for the remaining nineteen hours he was quietly and decently drunk. During the eight weeks I spent with him on Oolong Atoll, I never saw him draw a sober breath. In fact, his sleep was so short that he never had time to sober up. It was the most beautiful and orderly perennial drunk I have ever observed.

McAllister was his name. He was an old man, and very shaky on his pins. His hand trembled as with a palsy, especially noticeable when he poured his whiskey, though I never knew him to spill a drop. He had been twenty-eight years in Melanesia, ranging from German New Guinea to the German Solomons, and so thoroughly had he become identified with that portion of the world, that he habitually spoke in that bastard lingo called "bêche-de-mer." Thus, in conversation with me, *sun he come up* meant sunrise; *kai-kai he stop* meant that dinner was served; and *belly belong me walk about* meant that he was sick at his stomach. He was a small man, and a withered one, burned inside and outside by ardent spirits and ardent sun. He was a cinder, a bit of a clinker of a man, a little animated clinker, not yet quite cold, that moved stiffly and by starts and jerks like an automaton. A gust of wind would have blown him away. He weighed ninety pounds.

But the immense thing about him was the power with which

50

he ruled. Oolong Atoll was one hundred and forty miles in circumference. One steered by compass course in its lagoon. It was populated by five thousand Polynesians, all strapping men and women, many of them standing six feet in height and weighing a couple of hundred pounds. Oolong was two hundred and fifty miles from the nearest land. Twice a year a little schooner called to collect copra. The one white man on Oolong was McAllister, petty trader and unintermittent guzzler; and he ruled Oolong and its six thousand savages with an iron hand. He said come, and they came, go, and they went. They never questioned his will nor judgment. He was cantankerous as only an aged Scotchman can be, and interfered continually in their personal affairs. When Nugu, the king's daughter, wanted to marry Haunau from the other end of the atoll, her father said yes; but McAllister said no, and the marriage never came off. When the king wanted to buy a certain islet in the lagoon from the chief priest, McAllister said no. The king was in debt to the Company to the tune of 180,000 cocoanuts, and until that was paid he was not to spend a single cocoanut on anything else.

And yet the king and his people did not love McAllister. In truth, they hated him horribly, and, to my knowledge, the whole population, with the priests at the head, tried vainly for three months to pray him to death. The devil-devils they sent after him were awe-inspiring, but since McAllister did not believe in devil-devils, they were without power over him. With drunken Scotchmen all signs fail. They gathered up scraps of food which had touched his lips, an empty whiskey bottle, a cocoanut from which he had drunk, and even his spittle, and performed all kinds of deviltries over them. But McAllister lived on. His health was superb. He never caught fever; nor coughs nor colds; dysentery passed him by; and the malignant ulcers and vile skin diseases that attack blacks and whites alike in that climate never fastened upon him. He must have been so saturated with alcohol as to defy the lodgment of germs. I used to imagine them falling to the ground in showers of microscopic cinders as fast as they entered his whiskey-sodden aura. No one loved him, not even germs, while he loved only whiskey, and still he lived.

I was puzzled. I could not understand six thousand natives

putting up with that withered shrimp of a tyrant. It was a miracle that he had not died suddenly long since. Unlike the cowardly Melanesians, the people were high-stomached and warlike. In the big graveyard, at head and feet of the graves, were relics of past sanguinary history—blubber-spades, rusty old bayonets and cutlasses, copper bolts, rudder-irons, harpoons, bomb guns, bricks that could have come from nowhere but a whaler's trying-out furnace, and old brass pieces of the sixteenth century that verified the traditions of the early Spanish navigators. Ship after ship had come to grief on Oolong. Not thirty years before, the whaler *Blennerdale*, running into the lagoon for repairs, had been cut off with all hands. In similar fashion had the crew of the *Gasket*, a sandalwood trader, perished. There was a big French bark, the *Toulon*, becalmed off the atoll, which the islanders boarded after a sharp tussle and wrecked in the Lipau Passage, the captain and a handful of sailors escaping in the longboat. Then there were the Spanish pieces, which told of the loss of one of the early explorers. All this, of the vessels named, is a matter of history, and is to be found in the *South Pacific Sailing Directory*. But that there was other history, unwritten, I was yet to learn. In the meantime I puzzled why six thousand primitive savages let one degenerate Scotch despot live.

One hot afternoon McAllister and I sat on the veranda looking out over the lagoon, with all its wonder of jewelled colors. At our backs, across the hundred yards of palm-studded sand, the outer surf roared on the reef. It was dreadfully warm. We were in 4° south latitude and the sun was directly overhead, having crossed the Line a few days before on its journey south. There was no wind—not even a catspaw. The season of the southeast trade was drawing to an early close, and the northwest monsoon had not yet begun to blow.

"They can't dance worth a damn," said McAllister.

I had happened to mention that the Polynesian dances were superior to the Papuan, and this McAllister had denied, for no other reason than his cantankerousness. But it was too hot to argue, and I said nothing. Besides, I had never seen the Oolong people dance.

"I'll prove it to you," he announced, beckoning to the black New Hanover boy, a labor recruit, who served as cook and general house servant. "Hey, you, boy, you tell 'm one fella king come along me."

The boy departed, and back came the prime minister, perturbed, ill at ease, and garrulous with apologetic explanation. In short, the king slept, and was not to be disturbed.

"King he plenty strong fella sleep," was his final sentence.

McAllister was in such a rage that the prime minister incontinently fled, to return with the king himself. They were a magnificent pair, the king especially, who must have been all of six feet three inches in height. His features had the eagle-like quality that is so frequently found in those of the North American Indian. He had been both moulded and born to rule. His eyes flashed as he listened, but right meekly he obeyed McAllister's command to fetch a couple of hundred of the best dancers, male and female, in the village. And dance they did, for two mortal hours, under that broiling sun. They did not love him for it, and little he cared, in the end dismissing them with abuse and sneers.

The abject servility of those magnificent savages was terrifying. How could it be? What was the secret of his rule? More and more I puzzled as the days went by, and though I observed perpetual examples of his undisputed sovereignty, never a clew was there as to how it was.

One day I happened to speak of my disappointment in failing to trade for a beautiful pair of orange cowries. The pair was worth five pounds in Sydney if it was worth a cent. I had offered two hundred sticks of tobacco to the owner, who had held out for three hundred. When I casually mentioned the situation, McAllister immediately sent for the man, took the shells from him, and turned them over to me. Fifty sticks were all he permitted me to pay for them. The man accepted the tobacco and seemed overjoyed at getting off so easily. As for me, I resolved to keep a bridle on my tongue in the future. And still I mulled over the secret of McAllister's power. I even went to the extent of asking him directly, but all he did was to cock one eye, look wise, and take another drink.

One night I was out fishing in the lagoon with Oti, the man
who had been mulcted of the cowries. Privily, I had made up to
him an additional hundred and fifty sticks, and he had come to
regard me with a respect that was almost veneration, which was
curious, seeing that he was an old man, twice my age at least.

"What name you fella kanaka all the same pickaninny?" I
began on him. "This fella trader he one fella. You fella kanaka
plenty fella too much. You fella kanaka just like 'm dog—plenty
fright along that fella trader. He no eat you fella. He no get 'm
teeth along him. What name you too much fright?"

"S'pose plenty fella kanaka kill 'm?" he asked.

"He die," I retorted. "You fella kanaka kill 'm plenty fella
white man long time before. What name you fright this fella
white man?"

"Yes, we kill 'm plenty," was his answer. "My word! Any
amount! Long time before. One time, me young fella too much,
one big fella ship he stop outside. Wind he no blow. Plenty fella
kanaka we get 'm canoe, plenty fella canoe, we go catch 'm that
fella ship. My word—we catch 'm big fella fight. Two, three
white men shoot like hell. We no fright. We come alongside, we
go up side, plenty fella, maybe I think fifty-ten (five hundred).
One fella white Mary (woman) belong that fella ship. Never
before I see 'm white Mary. Bime by plenty white man finish.
One fella skipper he no die. Five fella, six fella white man no die.
Skipper he sing out. Some fella white man he fight. Some fella
white man he lower away boat. After that, all together over the
side they go. Skipper he sling white Mary down. After that they
washee (row) strong fella plenty too much. Father belong me,
that time he strong fella. He throw 'm one fella spear. That fella
spear he go in one side that white Mary. He no stop. My word,
he go out other side that fella Mary. She finish. Me no fright.
Plenty kanaka too much no fright."

Old Oti's pride had been touched, for he suddenly stripped
down his lava-lava and showed me the unmistakable scar of a
bullet. Before I could speak, his line ran out suddenly. He
checked it and attempted to haul in, but found that the fish had
run around a coral branch. Casting a look of reproach at me for
having beguiled him from his watchfulness, he went over the

side, feet first, turning over after he got under and following his line down to bottom. The water was ten fathoms. I leaned over and watched the play of his feet, growing dim and dimmer, as they stirred the wan phosphorescence into ghostly fires. Ten fathoms—sixty feet—it was nothing to him, an old man, compared with the value of a hook and line. After what seemed five minutes, though it could not have been more than a minute, I saw him flaming whitely upward. He broke surface and dropped a ten-pound rock cod into the canoe, the line and hook intact, the latter still fast in the fish's mouth.

"It may be," I said remorselessly. "You no fright long ago. You plenty fright now along that fella trader."

"Yes, plenty fright," he confessed, with an air of dismissing the subject. For half an hour we pulled up our lines and flung them out in silence. Then small fish-sharks began to bite, and after losing a hook apiece, we hauled in and waited for the sharks to go their way.

"I speak you true," Oti broke into speech, "then you savve we fright now."

I lighted up my pipe and waited, and the story that Oti told me in atrocious bêche-de-mer I here turn into proper English. Otherwise, in spirit and order of narrative, the tale is as it fell from Oti's lips.

"It was after that that we were very proud. We had fought many times with the strange white men who live upon the sea, and always we had beaten them. A few of us were killed, but what was that compared with the stores of wealth of a thousand thousand kinds that we found on the ships? And then one day, maybe twenty years ago, or twenty-five, there came a schooner right through the passage and into the lagoon. It was a large schooner with three masts. She had five white men and maybe forty boat's crew, black fellows from New Guinea and New Britain; and she had come to fish bêche-de-mer. She lay at anchor across the lagoon from here, at Pauloo, and her boats scattered out everywhere, making camps on the beaches where they cured the bêche-de-mer. This made them weak by dividing them, for those who fished here and those on the schooner at Pauloo were fifty miles apart, and there were others farther away still.

"Our king and headmen held council, and I was one in the canoe that paddled all afternoon and all night across the lagoon, bringing word to the people of Pauloo that in the morning we would attack the fishing camps at the one time and that it was for them to take the schooner. We who brought the word were tired with the paddling, but we took part in the attack. On the schooner were two white men, the skipper and the second mate, with half a dozen black boys. The skipper with three boys we caught on shore and killed, but first eight of us the skipper killed with his two revolvers. We fought close together, you see, at hand grapples.

"The noise of our fighting told the mate what was happening, and he put food and water and a sail in the small dingy, which was so small that it was no more than twelve feet long. We came down upon the schooner, a thousand men, covering the lagoon with our canoes. Also, we were blowing conch-shells, singing war-songs, and striking the sides of the canoes with our paddles. What chance had one white man and three black boys against us? No chance at all, and the mate knew it.

"White men are hell. I have watched them much, and I am an old man now, and I understand at last why the white men have taken to themselves all the islands in the sea. It is because they are hell. Here are you in the canoe with me. You are hardly more than a boy. You are not wise, for each day I tell you many things you do not know. When I was a little pickaninny, I knew more about fish and the ways of fish than you know now. I am an old man, but I swim down to the bottom of the lagoon, and you cannot follow me. What are you good for, anyway? I do not know, except to fight. I have never seen you fight, yet I know that you are like your brothers and that you will fight like hell. Also, you are a fool, like your brothers. You do not know when you are beaten. You will fight until you die, and then it will be too late to know that you are beaten.

"Now behold what this mate did. As we came down upon him, covering the sea and blowing our conches, he put off from the schooner in the small boat, along with the three black boys, and rowed for the passage. There again he was a fool, for no wise man would put out to sea in so small a boat. The sides of it were not four inches above the water. Twenty canoes went after him, filled with two hundred young men. We paddled five fathoms while his black boys were rowing one fathom. He had no chance, but he was a fool. He stood up in the boat with a rifle, and he shot many times. He was not a good shot, but as we drew close many of us were wounded and killed. But still he had no chance.

"I remember that all the time he was smoking a cigar. When we were forty feet away and coming fast, he dropped the rifle, lighted a stick of dynamite with the cigar, and threw it at us. He lighted another and another, and threw them at us very rapidly, many of them. I know now that he must have split the ends of the fuses and stuck in match-heads, because they lighted so quickly. Also, the fuses were very short. Sometimes the dynamite sticks went off in the air, but most of them went off in the canoes. And each time they went off in a canoe, that canoe was finished. Of the twenty canoes, the half were smashed to pieces. The canoe I was in was so smashed, and likewise the two men who sat next to me. The dynamite fell between them. The other canoes turned and ran away. Then that mate yelled, 'Yah! Yah! Yah!' at us. Also he went at us again with his rifle, so that many were killed through the back as they fled away. And all the time the black boys in the boat went on rowing. You see, I told you true, that mate was hell.

"Nor was that all. Before he left the schooner, he set her on fire, and fixed up all the powder and dynamite so that it would go off at one time. There were hundreds of us on board, trying to put out the fire, heaving up water from overside, when the schooner blew up. So that all we had fought for was lost to us, besides many more of us being killed. Sometimes, even now, in my old age, I have bad dreams in which I hear that mate yell, 'Yah! Yah! Yah!' In a voice of thunder he yells, 'Yah! Yah! Yah!' But all those in the fishing camps were killed.

"The mate went out of the passage in his little boat, and that was the end of him we made sure, for how could so small a boat, with four men in it, live on the ocean? A month went by, and then, one morning, between two rain squalls, a schooner sailed in through our passage and dropped anchor before the village.

The king and the headmen made big talk, and it was agreed that we would take the schooner in two or three days. In the meantime, as it was our custom always to appear friendly, we went off to her in canoes, bringing strings of cocoanuts, fowls, and pigs, to trade. But when we were alongside, many canoes of us, the men on board began to shoot us with rifles, and as we paddled away I saw the mate who had gone to sea in the little boat spring upon the rail and dance and yell, 'Yah! Yah! Yah!'

"That afternoon they landed from the schooner in three small boats filled with white men. They went right through the village, shooting every man they saw. Also they shot the fowls and pigs. We who were not killed got away in canoes and paddled out into the lagoon. Looking back, we could see all the houses on fire. Late in the afternoon we saw many canoes coming from Nihi, which is the village near the Nihi Passage in the northeast. They were all that were left, and like us their village had been burned by a second schooner that had come through Nihi Passage.

"We stood on in the darkness to the westward for Pauloo, but in the middle of the night we heard women wailing and then we ran into a big fleet of canoes. They were all that were left of Pauloo, which likewise was in ashes, for a third schooner had come in through the Pauloo Passage. You see, that mate, with his black boys, had not been drowned. He had made the Solomon Islands, and there told his brothers of what we had done in Oolong. And all his brothers had said they would come and punish us, and there they were in the three schooners, and our three villages were wiped out.

"And what was there for us to do? In the morning the two schooners from windward sailed down upon us in the middle of the lagoon. The trade-wind was blowing fresh, and by scores of canoes they ran us down. And the rifles never ceased talking. We scattered like flying-fish before the bonita, and there were so many of us that we escaped by thousands, this way and that, to the islands on the rim of the atoll.

"And thereafter the schooners hunted us up and down the lagoon. In the nighttime we slipped past them. But the next day, or in two days or three days, the schooners would be coming back, hunting us toward the other end of the lagoon. And so it went. We no longer counted nor remembered our dead. True, we were many and they were few. But what could we do? I was in one of the twenty canoes filled with men who were not afraid to die. We attacked the smallest schooner. They shot us down in heaps. They threw dynamite into the canoes, and when the dynamite gave out, they threw hot water down upon us. And the rifles never ceased talking. And those whose canoes were smashed were shot as they swam away. And the mate danced up and down upon the cabin-top and yelled, 'Yah! Yah! Yah!'

"Every house on every smallest island was burned. Not a pig nor a fowl was left alive. Our wells were defiled with the bodies of the slain, or else heaped high with coral rock. We were twenty-five thousand on Oolong before the three schooners came. To-day we are five thousand. After the schooners left, we were but three thousand, as you shall see.

"At last the three schooners grew tired of chasing us back and forth. So they went, the three of them, to Nihi, in the northeast. And then they drove us steadily to the west. Their nine boats were in the water as well. They beat up every island as they moved along. They drove us, drove us, drove us day by day. And every night the three schooners and the nine boats made a chain of watchfulness that stretched across the lagoon from rim to rim, so that we could not escape back.

"They could not drive us forever that way, for the lagoon was only so large, and at last all of us that yet lived were driven upon the last sand-bank to the west. Beyond lay the open sea. There were ten thousand of us, and we covered the sand-bank from the lagoon edge to the pounding surf on the other side. No one could lie down. There was no room. We stood hip to hip and shoulder to shoulder. Two days they kept us there, and the mate would climb up in the rigging to mock us and yell, 'Yah! Yah! Yah!' till we were well sorry that we had ever harmed him or his schooner a month before. We had no food, and we stood on our feet two days and nights. The little babies died, and the old and weak died, and the wounded died. And worst of all, we had no water to quench our thirst, and for two days the sun beat down on us, and there was no shade. Many men and women waded out into the ocean and were drowned, the surf casting their bod-

ies back on the beach. And there came a pest of flies. Some men
swam to the sides of the schooners, but they were shot to the
last one. And we that lived were very sorry that in our pride we
tried to take the schooner with the three masts that came to fish
for bêche-de-mer.

"On the morning of the third day came the skippers of the
three schooners and that mate in a small boat. They carried
rifles, all of them, and revolvers, and they made talk. It was only
that they were weary of killing us that they had stopped, they
told us. And we told them that we were sorry, that never again
would we harm a white man, and in token of our submission we
poured sand upon our heads. And all the women and children
set up a great wailing for water, so that for some time no man
could make himself heard. Then we were told our punishment.
We must fill the three schooners with copra and bêche-de-mer.
And we agreed, for we wanted water, and our hearts were broken, and we knew that we were children at fighting when we
fought with white men who fight like hell. And when all the talk
was finished, the mate stood up and mocked us, and yelled,
'Yah! Yah! Yah!' After that we paddled away in our canoes and
sought water.

"And for weeks we toiled at catching bêche-de-mer and cur-
ing it, in gathering the cocoanuts and turning them into copra.
By day and night the smoke rose in clouds from all the beaches
of all the islands of Oolong as we paid the penalty of our wrong-
doing. For in those days of death it was burned clearly on all our
brains that it was very wrong to harm a white man.

"By and by, the schooners full of copra and bêche-de-mer and
our trees empty of cocoanuts, the three skippers and that mate
called us all together for a big talk. And they said they were very
glad that we had learned our lesson, and we said for the ten-
thousandth time that we were sorry and that we would not do it
again. Also, we poured sand upon our heads. Then the skippers
said that it was all very well, but just to show us that they did not
forget us, they would send a devil-devil that we would never forget and that we would always remember any time we might feel
like harming a white man. After that the mate mocked us one
more time and yelled, 'Yah! Yah! Yah!' Then six of our men,

whom we thought long dead, were put ashore from one of the schooners, and the schooners hoisted their sails and ran out through the passage for the Solomons.

"The six men who were put ashore were the first to catch the devil-devil the skippers sent back after us."

"A great sickness came," I interrupted, for I recognized the trick. The schooner had had measles on board, and the six prisoners had been deliberately exposed to it.

"Yes, a great sickness," Oti went on. "It was a powerful devil-devil. The oldest man had never heard of the like. Those of our priests that yet lived we killed because they could not overcome the devil-devil. The sickness spread. I have said that there were ten thousand of us that stood hip to hip and shoulder to shoulder on the sand-bank. When the sickness left us, there were three thousand yet alive. Also, having made all our cocoanuts into copra, there was a famine.

"That fella trader," Oti concluded, "he like 'm that much dirt. He like 'm clam he die *kai-kai* (meat) he stop, stink 'm any amount. He like 'm one fella dog, one sick fella dog plenty fleas stop along him. We no fright along that fella trader. We fright because he white man. We savve plenty too much no good kill white man. That one fella sick dog trader he plenty brother stop along him, white men like 'm you fight like hell. We no fright that damn trader. Some time he made kanaka plenty cross along him and kanaka want 'm kill 'm, kanaka he think devil-devil and kanaka he hear that fella mate sing out, 'Yah! Yah! Yah!' and kanaka no kill 'm."

Oti baited his hook with a piece of squid, which he tore with his teeth from the live and squirming monster, and hook and bait sank in white flames to the bottom.

"Shark walk about he finish," he said. "I think we catch 'm plenty fella fish."

His line jerked savagely. He pulled it in rapidly, hand under hand, and landed a big gasping rock cod in the bottom of the canoe.

"Sun he come up, I make 'm that dam fella trader one present big fella fish," said Oti.

The Heathen

I met him first in a hurricane; and though we had gone through the hurricane on the same schooner, it was not until the schooner had gone to pieces under us that I first laid eyes on him. Without doubt I had seen him with the rest of the kanaka crew on board, but I had not consciously been aware of his existence, for the *Petite Jeanne* was rather overcrowded. In addition to her eight or ten kanaka seamen, her white captain, mate, and supercargo, and her six cabin passengers, she sailed from Rangiroa with something like eighty-five deck passengers—Paumotans and Tahitians, men, women, and children each with a trade box, to say nothing of sleeping-mats, blankets, and clothes-bundles.

The pearling season in the Paumotus was over, and all hands were returning to Tahiti. The six of us cabin passengers were pearl-buyers. Two were Americans, one was Ah Choon (the whitest Chinese I have ever known), one was a German, one was a Polish Jew, and I completed the half dozen.

It had been a prosperous season. Not one of us had cause for complaint, nor one of the eighty-five deck passengers either. All had done well, and all were looking forward to a rest-off and a good time in Papeete.

Of course, the *Petite Jeanne* was overloaded. She was only seventy tons, and she had no right to carry a tithe of the mob she had on board. Beneath her hatches she was crammed and jammed with pearl-shell and copra. Even the trade room was packed full with shell. It was a miracle that the sailors could work her. There was no moving about the decks. They simply climbed back and forth along the rails.

62

In the night-time they walked upon the sleepers, who carpeted the deck, I'll swear, two deep. Oh! and there were pigs and chickens on deck, and sacks of yams, while every conceivable place was festooned with strings of drinking cocoanuts and bunches of bananas. On both sides, between the fore and main shrouds, guys had been stretched, just low enough for the foreboom to swing clear; and from each of these guys at least fifty bunches of bananas were suspended.

It promised to be a messy passage, even if we did make it in the two or three days that would have been required if the southeast trades had been blowing fresh. But they weren't blowing fresh. After the first five hours the trade died away in a dozen or so gasping fans. The calm continued all that night and the next day—one of those glaring, glassy, calms, when the very thought of opening one's eyes to look at it is sufficient to cause a headache.

The second day a man died—an Easter Islander, one of the best divers that season in the lagoon. Smallpox—that is what it was; though how smallpox could come on board, when there had been no known cases ashore when we left Rangiroa, is beyond me. There it was, though—smallpox, a man dead, and three others down on their backs.

There was nothing to be done. We could not segregate the sick, nor could we care for them. We were packed like sardines. There was nothing to do but rot and die—that is, there was nothing to do after the night that followed the first death. On that night, the mate, the supercargo, the Polish Jew, and four native divers sneaked away in the large whale-boat. They were never heard of again. In the morning the captain promptly scuttled the remaining boats, and there we were.

That day there were two deaths; the following day three; then it jumped to eight. It was curious to see how we took it. The natives, for instance, fell into a condition of dumb, stolid fear. The captain—Oudouse, his name was, a Frenchman—became very nervous and voluble. He actually got the twitches. He was a large, fleshy man, weighing at least two hundred pounds, and he quickly became a faithful representation of a quivering jelly-mountain of fat.

The German, the two Americans, and myself bought up all the Scotch whiskey, and proceeded to stay drunk. The theory was beautiful—namely, if we kept ourselves soaked in alcohol, every smallpox germ that came into contact with us would immediately be scorched to a cinder. And the theory worked, though I must confess that neither Captain Oudouse nor Ah Choon were attacked by the disease either. The Frenchman did not drink at all, while Ah Choon restricted himself to one drink daily.

It was a pretty time. The sun, going into northern declination, was straight overhead. There was no wind, except for frequent squalls, which blew fiercely for from five minutes to half an hour, and wound up by deluging us with rain. After each squall, the awful sun would come out, drawing clouds of steam from the soaked decks.

The steam was not nice. It was the vapor of death, freighted with millions and millions of germs. We always took another drink when we saw it going up from the dead and dying, and usually we took two or three more drinks, mixing them exceptionally stiff. Also, we made it a rule to take an additional several each time they hove the dead over to the sharks that swarmed about us.

We had a week of it, and then the whiskey gave out. It is just as well, or I shouldn't be alive now. It took a sober man to pull through what followed, as you will agree when I mention the little fact that only two men did pull through. The other man was the heathen—at least, that was what I heard Captain Oudouse call him at the moment I first became aware of the heathen's existence. But to come back.

It was at the end of the week, with the whiskey gone, and the pearl-buyers sober, that I happened to glance at the barometer that hung in the cabin companionway. Its normal register in the Paumotus was 29.90, and it was quite customary to see it vacillate between 29.85 and 30.00, or even 30.05; but to see it as I saw it, down to 29.62, was sufficient to sober the most drunken pearl-buyer that ever incinerated smallpox microbes in Scotch whiskey.

I called Captain Oudouse's attention to it, only to be informed that he had watched it going down for several hours. There was little to do, but that little he did very well, considering the circumstances. He took off the light sails, shortened right down to storm canvas, spread life-lines, and waited for the wind. His mistake lay in what he did after the wind came. He hove to on the port tack, which was the right thing to do south of the Equator, if—and there was the rub—*if* one were *not* in the direct path of the hurricane.

We were in the direct path. I could see that by the steady increase of the wind and the equally steady fall of the barometer. I wanted him to turn and run with the wind on the port quarter until the barometer ceased falling, and then to heave to. We argued till he was reduced to hysteria, but budge he would not. The worst of it was that I could not get the rest of the pearl-buyers to back me up. Who was I, anyway, to know more about the sea and its ways than a properly qualified captain? was what was in their minds, I knew.

Of course the sea rose with the wind frightfully; and I shall never forget the first three seas the *Petite Jeanne* shipped. She had fallen off, as vessels do at times when hove to, and the first sea made a clean breach. The life-lines were only for the strong and well, and little good were they even for them when the women and children, the bananas and cocoanuts, the pigs and trade boxes, the sick and the dying, were swept along in a solid, screeching, groaning mass.

The second sea filled the *Petite Jeanne's* decks flush with the rails; and, as her stern sank down and her bow tossed skyward, all the miserable dunnage of life and luggage poured aft. It was a human torrent. They came head-first, feet-first, sidewise, rolling over and over, twisting, squirming, writhing, and crumpling up. Now and again one caught a grip on a stanchion or a rope; but the weight of the bodies behind tore such grips loose.

One man I noticed fetch up, head on and square on, with the starboard-bitt. His head cracked like an egg. I saw what was coming, sprang on top of the cabin, and from there into the mainsail itself. Ah Choon and one of the Americans tried to follow me, but I was one jump ahead of them. The American was swept away and over the stern like a piece of chaff. Ah Choon caught a spoke of the wheel, and swung in behind it. But a strapping Raratonga vahine (woman)—she must have weighed two hundred and fifty—brought up against him, and got an arm around his neck. He clutched the kanaka steersman with his other hand; and just at that moment the schooner flung down to starboard.

The rush of bodies and sea that was coming along the port runway between the cabin and the rail turned abruptly and poured to starboard. Away they went—vahine, Ah Choon, and steersman; and I swear I saw Ah Choon grin at me with philosophic resignation as he cleared the rail and went under.

The third sea—the biggest of the three—did not do so much damage. By the time it arrived nearly everybody was in the rigging. On deck perhaps a dozen gasping, half-drowned, and half-stunned wretches were rolling about or attempting to crawl into safety. They went by the board, as did the wreckage of the two remaining boats. The other pearl-buyers and myself, between seas, managed to get about fifteen women and children into the cabin, and battened down. Little good it did the poor creatures in the end.

Wind? Out of all my experience I could not have believed it possible for the wind to blow as it did. There is no describing it. How can one describe a nightmare? It was the same way with that wind. It tore the clothes off our bodies. I say *tore them off*, and I mean it. I am not asking you to believe it. I am merely telling something that I saw and felt. There are times when I do not believe it myself. I went through it, and that is enough. One could not face that wind and live. It was a monstrous thing, and the most monstrous thing about it was that it increased and continued to increase.

Imagine countless millions and billions of tons of sand. Imagine this sand tearing along at ninety, a hundred, a hundred and twenty, or any other number of miles per hour. Imagine, further, this sand to be invisible, impalpable, yet to retain all the weight and density of sand. Do all this, and you may get a vague inkling of what that wind was like.

Perhaps sand is not the right comparison. Consider it mud, invisible, impalpable, but heavy as mud. Nay, it goes beyond that. Consider every molecule of air to be a mud-bank in itself. Then try to imagine the multitudinous impact of mud-banks. No; it is beyond me. Language may be adequate to express the ordinary conditions of life, but it cannot possibly express any of the conditions of so enormous a blast of wind. It would have been better had I stuck by my original intention of not attempting a description.

I will say this much: The sea, which had risen at first, was beaten down by that wind. More: it seemed as if the whole ocean had been sucked up in the maw of the hurricane, and hurled on through that portion of space which previously had been occupied by the air.

Of course, our canvas had gone long before. But Captain Oudouse had on the *Petite Jeanne* something I had never before seen on a South Sea schooner—a sea-anchor. It was a conical canvas bag, the mouth of which was kept open by a huge hoop of iron. The sea-anchor was bridled something like a kite, so that it bit into the water as a kite bites into the air, but with a difference. The sea-anchor remained just under the surface of the ocean in a perpendicular position. A long line, in turn, connected it with the schooner. As a result, the *Petite Jeanne* rode bow on to the wind and to what sea there was.

The situation really would have been favorable had we not been in the path of the storm. True, the wind itself tore our canvas out of the gaskets, jerked out our topmasts, and made a raffle of our running-gear, but still we would have come through nicely had we not been square in front of the advancing storm-centre. That was what fixed us. I was in a state of stunned, numbed, paralysed collapse from enduring the impact of the wind, and I think I was just about ready to give up and die when the centre smote us. The blow we received was an absolute lull. There was not a breath of air. The effect on one was sickening.

Remember that for hours we had been at terrific muscular tension, withstanding the awful pressure of that wind. And then, suddenly, the pressure was removed. I know that I felt as though I was about to expand, to fly apart in all directions. It seemed as if every atom composing my body was repelling every other atom and was on the verge of rushing off irresistibly into space. But that lasted only for a moment. Destruction was upon us.

In the absence of the wind and pressure the sea rose. It jumped, it leaped, it soared straight toward the clouds. Remember, from every point of the compass that inconceivable wind was blowing in toward the centre of calm. The result was that the seas sprang up from every point of the compass. There was no wind to check them. They popped up like corks released from the bottom of a pail of water. There was no system to them, no stability. They were hollow, maniacal seas. They were eighty feet high at the least. They were not seas at all. They resembled no sea a man had ever seen.

They were splashes, monstrous splashes—that is all. Splashes that were eighty feet high. Eighty! They were more than eighty. They went over our mastheads. They were spouts, explosions. They were drunken. They fell anywhere, anyhow. They jostled one another; they collided. They rushed together and collapsed upon one another, or fell apart like a thousand waterfalls all at once. It was no ocean any man had ever dreamed of, that hurricane centre. It was confusion thrice confounded. It was anarchy. It was a hell-pit of seawater gone mad.

The *Petite Jeanne?* I don't know. The heathen told me afterwards that he did not know. She was literally torn apart, ripped wide open, beaten into a pulp, smashed into kindling wood, annihilated. When I came to I was in the water, swimming automatically, though I was about two-thirds drowned. How I got there I had no recollection. I remembered seeing the *Petite Jeanne* fly to pieces at what must have been the instant that my own consciousness was buffeted out of me. But there I was, with nothing to do but make the best of it, and in that best there was little promise. The wind was blowing again, the sea was much smaller and more regular, and I knew that I had passed through the centre. Fortunately, there were no sharks about. The hurricane had dissipated the ravenous horde that had surrounded the death ship and fed off the dead.

It was about midday when the *Petite Jeanne* went to pieces, and it must have been two hours afterwards when I picked up with one of her hatch-covers. Thick rain was driving at the time;

and it was the merest chance that flung me and the hatch-cover together. A short length of line was trailing from the rope handle; and I knew that I was good for a day, at least, if the sharks did not return. Three hours later, possibly a little longer, sticking close to the cover, and, with closed eyes, concentrating my whole soul upon the task of breathing in enough air to keep me going and at the same time of avoiding breathing in enough water to drown me, it seemed to me that I heard voices. The rain had ceased, and wind and sea were easing marvellously. Not twenty feet away from me, on another hatch-cover, were Captain Oudouse and the heathen. They were fighting over the possession of the cover—at least, the Frenchman was.

"Païen noir!" I heard him scream, and at the same time I saw him kick the kanaka.

Now, Captain Oudouse had lost all his clothes, except his shoes, and they were heavy brogans. It was a cruel blow, for it caught the heathen on the mouth and the point of the chin, half stunning him. I looked for him to retaliate, but he contented himself with swimming about forlornly a safe ten feet away. Whenever a fling of the sea threw him closer, the Frenchman, hanging on with his hands, kicked out at him with both feet. Also, at the moment of delivering each kick, he called the kanaka a black heathen.

"For two centimes I'd come over there and drown you, you white beast!" I yelled.

The only reason I did not go was that I felt too tired. The very thought of the effort to swim over was nauseating. So I called to the kanaka to come to me, and proceeded to share the hatch-cover with him. Otoo, he told me his name was (pronounced ō-tō-ō); also, he told me that he was a native of Bora Bora, the most westerly of the Society Group. As I learned afterward, he had got the hatch-cover first, and, after some time, encountering Captain Oudouse, had offered to share it with him, and had been kicked off for his pains.

And that was how Otoo and I first came together. He was no fighter. He was all sweetness and gentleness, a love-creature, though he stood nearly six feet tall and was muscled like a gladiator. He was no fighter, but he was also no coward. He had the

heart of a lion; and in the years that followed I have seen him
run risks that I would never dream of taking. What I mean is
that while he was no fighter, and while he always avoided pre-
cipitating a row, he never ran away from trouble when it started.
And it was "'Ware shoal!" when once Otoo went into action. I
shall never forget what he did to Bill King. It occurred in
German Samoa. Bill King was hailed the champion heavyweight
of the American Navy. He was a big brute of a man, a veritable
gorilla, one of those hard-hitting, rough-housing chaps, and
clever with his fists as well. He picked the quarrel, and he
kicked Otoo twice and struck him once before Otoo felt it to be
necessary to fight. I don't think it lasted four minutes, at the end
of which time Bill King was the unhappy possessor of four broken ribs, a broken forearm, and a dislocated shoulder-blade.
Otoo knew nothing of scientific boxing. He was merely a manhandler; and Bill King was something like three months in
recovering from the bit of manhandling he received that afternoon on Apia beach.

But I am running ahead of my yarn. We shared the hatch-
cover between us. We took turn and turn about, one lying flat on
the cover and resting, while the other, submerged to the neck,
merely held on with his hands. For two days and nights, spell and
spell, on the cover and in the water, we drifted over the ocean.
Towards the last I was delirious most of the time; and there were
times, too, when I heard Otoo babbling and raving in his native
tongue. Our continuous immersion prevented us from dying of
thirst, though the sea-water and the sunshine gave us the preti-
est imaginable combination of salt pickle and sunburn.

In the end, Otoo saved my life; for I came to lying on the
beach twenty feet from the water, sheltered from the sun by a
couple of cocoanut leaves. No one but Otoo could have dragged
me there and stuck up the leaves for shade. He was lying beside
me. I went off again; and the next time I came round, it was cool
and starry night, and Otoo was pressing a drinking cocoanut to
my lips.

We were the sole survivors of the *Petite Jeanne*. Captain
Oudouse must have succumbed to exhaustion, for several days
later his hatch-cover drifted ashore without him. Otoo and I

lived with the natives of the atoll for a week, when we were res-
cued by the French cruiser and taken to Tahiti. In the meantime, however, we had performed the ceremony of exchanging
names. In the South Seas such a ceremony binds two men
closer together than blood-brothership. The initiative had been
mine; and Otoo was rapturously delighted when I suggested it.

"It is well," he said, in Tahitian. "For we have been mates
together for two days on the lips of Death."

"But Death stuttered," I smiled.

"It was a brave deed you did, master," he replied, "and Death
was not vile enough to speak."

"Why do you 'master' me?" I demanded, with a show of hurt
feelings. "We have exchanged names. To you I am Otoo. To me
you are Charley. And between you and me, forever and forever,
you shall be Charley, and I shall be Otoo. It is the way of the custom. And when we die, if it does happen that we live again
somewhere beyond the stars and the sky, still shall you be
Charley to me, and I Otoo to you."

"Yes, master," he answered, his eyes luminous and soft with
joy.

"There you go!" I cried indignantly.

"What does it matter what my lips utter?" he argued. "They
are only my lips. But I shall think Otoo always. Whenever I
think of myself, I shall think of you. Whenever men call me by
name, I shall think of you. And beyond the sky and beyond the
stars, always and forever, you shall be Otoo to me. Is it well,
master?"

I hid my smile, and answered that it was well.

We parted at Papeete. I remained ashore to recuperate; and
he went on in a cutter to his own island, Bora Bora. Six weeks
later he was back. I was surprised, for he had told me of his wife,
and said that he was returning to her, and would give over sailing on far voyages.

"Where do you go, master?" he asked, after our first greet-
ings.

I shrugged my shoulders. It was a hard question.

"All the world," was my answer—"all the world, all the sea,
and all the islands that are in the sea."

"I will go with you," he said simply. "My wife is dead."

I never had a brother; but from what I have seen of other men's brothers, I doubt if any man ever had a brother that was to him what Otoo was to me. He was brother and father and mother as well. And this I know: I lived a straighter and better man because of Otoo. I cared little for other men, but I had to live straight in Otoo's eyes. Because of him I dared not tarnish myself. He made me his ideal, compounding me, I fear, chiefly out of his own love and worship; and there were times when I stood close to the steep pitch of hell, and would have taken the plunge had not the thought of Otoo restrained me. His pride in me entered into me, until it became one of the major rules in my personal code to do nothing that would diminish that pride of his.

Naturally, I did not learn right away what his feelings were toward me. He never criticised, never censured; and slowly the exalted place I held in his eyes dawned upon me, and slowly I grew to comprehend the hurt I could inflict upon him by being anything less than my best.

For seventeen years we were together; for seventeen years he was at my shoulder, watching while I slept, nursing me through fever and wounds—ay, and receiving wounds in fighting for me. He signed on the same ships with me; and together we ranged the Pacific from Hawaii to Sydney Head, and from Torres Straits to the Galapagos. We blackbirded from the New Hebrides and the Line Islands over to the westward clear through the Louisades, New Britain, New Ireland, and New Hanover. We were wrecked three times—in the Gilberts, in the Santa Cruz group, and in the Fijis. And we traded and salved wherever a dollar promised in the way of pearl and pearl-shell, copra, bêche-de-mer, hawkbill turtle-shell, and stranded wrecks.

It began in Papeete, immediately after his announcement that he was going with me over all the sea, and the islands in the midst thereof. There was a club in those days in Papeete, where the pearlers, traders, captains, and riffraff of South Sea adventurers forgathered. The play ran high, and the drink ran high; and I am very much afraid that I kept later hours than were becoming or proper. No matter what the hour was when I left the club, there was Otoo waiting to see me safely home.

At first I smiled; next I chided him. Then I told him flatly that I stood in need of no wet-nursing. After that I did not see him when I came out of the club. Quite by accident, a week or so later, I discovered that he still saw me home, lurking across the street among the shadows of the mango-trees. What could I do? I know what I did do.

Insensibly I began to keep better hours. On wet and stormy nights, in the thick of the folly and the fun, the thought would persist in coming to me of Otoo keeping his dreary vigil under the dripping mangoes. Truly, he made a better man of me. Yet he was not strait-laced. And he knew nothing of common Christian morality. All the people on Bora Bora were Christians; but he was a heathen, the only unbeliever on the island, a gross materialist, who believed that when he died he was dead. He believed merely in fair play and square dealing. Petty meanness, in his code, was almost as serious as wanton homicide; and I do believe that he respected a murderer more than a man given to small practices.

Concerning me, personally, he objected to my doing anything that was hurtful to me. Gambling was all right. He was an ardent gambler himself. But late hours, he explained, were bad for one's health. He had seen men who did not take care of themselves die of fever. He was no teetotaller, and welcomed a stiff nip any time when it was wet work in the boats. On the other hand, he believed in liquor in moderation. He had seen many men killed or disgraced by square-face or Scotch.

Otoo had my welfare always at heart. He thought ahead for me, weighed my plans, and took a greater interest in them than I did myself. At first, when I was unaware of this interest of his in my affairs, he had to divine my intentions, as, for instance, at Papeete, when I contemplated going partners with a knavish fellow-countryman on a guano venture. I did not know he was a knave. Nor did any white man in Papeete. Neither did Otoo know, but he saw how thick we were getting, and found out for me, and without my asking him. Native sailors from the ends of the seas knock about on the beach in Tahiti; and Otoo, suspi-

cious merely, went among them till he had gathered sufficient
data to justify his suspicions. Oh, it was a nice history, that of
Randolph Waters. I couldn't believe it when Otoo first narrated
it; but when I sheeted it home to Waters he gave in without a
murmur, and got away on the first steamer to Aukland.

At first, I am free to confess, I couldn't help resenting Otoo's
poking his nose into my business. But I knew that he was wholly
unselfish; and soon I had to acknowledge his wisdom and discre-
tion. He had his eyes open always to my main chance, and he was
both keen-sighted and far-sighted. In time he became my coun-
sellor, until he knew more of my business than I did myself. He
really had my interest at heart more than I did. Mine was the
magnificent carelessness of youth, for I preferred romance to
dollars, and adventure to a comfortable billet with all night in. So
it was well that I had some one to look out for me. I know that if
it had not been for Otoo, I should not be here to-day.

Of numerous instances, let me give one. I had had some
experience in blackbirding before I went pearling in the
Paumotus. Otoo and I were on the beach in Samoa—we really
were on the beach and hard aground—when my chance came
to go as recruiter on a blackbird brig. Otoo signed on before the
mast; and for the next half-dozen years, in as many ships, we
knocked about the wildest portions of Melanesia. Otoo saw to it
that he always pulled stroke-oar in my boat. Our custom in
recruiting labor was to land the recruiter on the beach. The covering boat always lay on its oars several hundred feet off shore,
while the recruiter's boat, also lying on its oars, kept afloat on
the edge of the beach. When I landed with my trade-goods,
leaving my steering sweep apeak, Otoo left his stroke position
and came into the stern-sheets, where a Winchester lay ready to
hand under a flap of canvas. The boat's crew was also armed, the
Sniders concealed under canvas flaps that ran the length of the
gunwales. While I was busy arguing and persuading the woolly-
headed cannibals to come and labor on the Queensland plantations Otoo kept watch. And often and often his low voice
warned me of suspicious actions and impending treachery.
Sometimes it was the quick shot from his rifle, knocking a nigger over, that was the first warning I received. And in my rush

to the boat his hand was always there to jerk me flying aboard. Once, I remember, on *Santa Anna,* the boat grounded just as the trouble began. The covering boat was dashing to our assistance, but the several score of savages would have wiped us out before it arrived. Otoo took a flying leap ashore, dug both hands into the trade-goods, and scattered tobacco, beads, tomahawks, knives, and calicoes in all directions.

This was too much for the woolly-heads. While they scrambled for the treasures, the boat was shoved clear, and we were aboard and forty feet away. And I got thirty recruits off that very beach in the next four hours.

The particular instance I have in mind was on Malaita, the most savage island in the easterly Solomons. The natives had been remarkably friendly; and how were we to know that the whole village had been taking up a collection for over two years with which to buy a white man's head? The beggars are all head-hunters, and they especially esteem a white man's head. The fellow who captured the head would receive the whole collection. As I say, they appeared very friendly; and on this day I was fully a hundred yards down the beach from the boat. Otoo had cautioned me; and, as usual when I did not heed him, I came to grief.

The first I knew, a cloud of spears sailed out of the mangrove swamp at me. At least a dozen were sticking into me. I started to run, but tripped over one that was fast in my calf, and went down. The woolly-heads made a run for me, each with a long-handled, fantail tomahawk with which to hack off my head. They were so eager for the prize that they got in one another's way. In the confusion, I avoided several hacks by throwing myself right and left on the sand.

Then Otoo arrived—Otoo the manhandler. In some way he had got hold of a heavy war club, and at close quarters it was a far more efficient weapon than a rifle. He was right in the thick of them, so that they could not spear him, while their tomahawks seemed worse than useless. He was fighting for me, and he was in a true Berserker rage. The way he handled that club was amazing. Their skulls squashed like overripe oranges. It was not until he had driven them back, picked me up in his arms, and started to run, that he received his first wounds. He arrived in the boat with four spear thrusts, got his Winchester, and with it got a man for every shot. Then we pulled aboard the schooner, and doctored up.

Seventeen years we were together. He made me. I should to-day be a supercargo, a recruiter, or a memory, if it had not been for him.

"You spend your money, and you go out and get more," he said one day. "It is easy to get money now. But when you get old, your money will be spent, and you will not be able to go out and get more. I know, master. I have studied the way of white men. On the beaches are many old men who were young once, and who could get money just like you. Now they are old, and they have nothing, and they wait about for the young men like you to come ashore and buy drinks for them.

"The black boy is a slave on the plantations. He gets twenty dollars a year. He works hard. The overseer does not work hard. He rides a horse and watches the black boy work. He gets twelve hundred dollars a year. I am a sailor on the schooner. I get fifteen dollars a month. That is because I am a good sailor. I work hard. The captain has a double awning, and drinks beer out of long bottles. I have never seen him haul a rope or pull an oar. He gets one hundred and fifty dollars a month. I am a sailor. He is a navigator. Master, I think it would be very good for you to know navigation."

Otoo spurred me on to it. He sailed with me as second mate on my first schooner, and he was far prouder of my command than I was myself. Later on it was:

"The captain is well paid, master; but the ship is in his keeping, and he is never free from the burden. It is the owner who is better paid—the owner who sits ashore with many servants and turns his money over."

"True, but a schooner costs five thousand dollars—an old schooner at that," I objected. "I should be an old man before I saved five thousand dollars."

"There be short ways for white men to make money," he went on, pointing ashore at the cocoanut-fringed beach.

We were in the Solomons at the time, picking up a cargo of ivory-nuts along the east coast of Guadalcanar.

"Between this river mouth and the next it is two miles," he said. "The flat land runs far back. It is worth nothing now. Next year—who knows?—or the year after, men will pay much money for that land. The anchorage is good. Big steamers can lie close up. You can buy the land four miles deep from the old chief for ten thousand sticks of tobacco, ten bottles of square-face, and a Snider, which will cost you, maybe, one hundred dollars. Then you place the deed with the commissioner; and the next year, or the year after, you sell and become the owner of a ship."

I followed his lead, and his words came true, though in three years, instead of two. Next came the grasslands deal on Guadalcanar—twenty thousand acres, on a governmental nine hundred and ninety-nine years' lease at a nominal sum. I owned the lease for precisely ninety days, when I sold it to a company for half a fortune. Always it was Otoo who looked ahead and saw the opportunity. He was responsible for the salving of the *Doncaster*—bought in at auction for a hundred pounds, and clearing three thousand after every expense was paid. He led me into the Savaii plantation and the cocoa venture on Upolu.

We did not go seafaring so much as in the old days. I was too well off. I married, and my standard of living rose; but Otoo remained the same old-time Otoo, moving about the house or trailing through the office, his wooden pipe in his mouth, a shilling undershirt on his back, and a four-shilling lava-lava about his loins. I could not get him to spend money. There was no way of repaying him except with love, and God knows he got that in full measure from all of us. The children worshipped him; and if he had been spoilable, my wife would surely have been his undoing.

The children! He really was the one who showed them the way of their feet in the world practical. He began by teaching them to walk. He sat up with them when they were sick. One by one, when they were scarcely toddlers, he took them down to the lagoon, and made them into amphibians. He taught them more than I ever knew of the habits of fish and the ways of catching them. In the bush it was the same thing. At seven, Tom knew more woodcraft than I ever dreamed existed. At six, Mary went over the Sliding Rock without a quiver, and I have seen strong men balk at that feat. And when Frank had just turned six he could bring up shillings from the bottom in three fathoms.

"My people in Bora Bora do not like heathen—they are all Christians; and I do not like Bora Bora Christians," he said one day, when I, with the idea of getting him to spend some of the money that was rightfully his, had been trying to persuade him to make a visit to his own island in one of our schooners—a special voyage which I had hoped to make a record breaker in the matter of prodigal expense.

I say one of *our* schooners, though legally at the time they belonged to me. I struggled long with him to enter into partnership.

"We have been partners from the day the *Petite Jeanne* went down," he said at last. "But if your heart so wishes, then shall we become partners by the law. I have no work to do, yet are my expenses large. I drink and eat and smoke in plenty—it costs much, I know. I do not pay for the playing of billiards, for I play on your table; but still the money goes. Fishing on the reef is only a rich man's pleasure. It is shocking, the cost of hooks and cotton line. Yes; it is necessary that we be partners by the law. I need the money. I shall get it from the head clerk in the office."

So the papers were made out and recorded. A year later I was compelled to complain.

"Charley," said I, "you are a wicked old fraud, a miserly skinflint, a miserable land-crab. Behold, your share for the year in all our partnership has been thousands of dollars. The head clerk has given me this paper. It says that in the year you have drawn just eighty-seven dollars and twenty cents."

"Is there any owing me?" he asked anxiously.

"I tell you thousands and thousands," I answered.

His face brightened, as with an immense relief.

"It is well," he said. "See that the head clerk keeps good account of it. When I want it, I shall want it, and there must not be a cent missing.

"If there is," he added fiercely, after a pause, "it must come out of the clerk's wages."

And all the time, as I afterwards learned, his will, drawn up by Carruthers, and making me sole beneficiary, lay in the American consul's safe.

But the end came, as the end must come to all human associations. It occurred in the Solomons, where our wildest work had been done in the wild young days, and where we were once more—principally on a holiday, incidentally to look after our holdings on Florida Island and to look over the pearling possibilities of the Mboli Pass. We were lying at Savo, having run in to trade for curios.

Now, Savo is alive with sharks. The custom of the woolly-heads of burying their dead in the sea did not tend to discourage the sharks from making the adjacent waters a hang-out. It was my luck to be coming aboard in a tiny, overloaded, native canoe, when the thing capsized. There were four woolly-heads and myself in it, or, rather, hanging to it. The schooner was a hundred yards away. I was just hailing for a boat when one of the woolly-heads began to scream. Holding on to the end of the canoe, both he and that portion of the canoe were dragged under several times. Then he loosed his clutch and disappeared. A shark had got him.

The three remaining niggers tried to climb out of the water upon the bottom of the canoe. I yelled and cursed and struck at the nearest with my fist, but it was no use. They were in a blind funk. The canoe could barely have supported one of them. Under the three it upended and rolled sidewise, throwing them back into the water.

I abandoned the canoe and started to swim toward the schooner, expecting to be picked up by the boat before I got there. One of the niggers elected to come with me, and we swam along silently, side by side, now and again putting our faces into the water and peering about for sharks. The screams of the man who stayed by the canoe informed us that he was taken. I was peering into the water when I saw a big shark pass directly beneath me. He was fully sixteen feet in length. I saw the whole thing. He got the woolly-head by the middle, and away he went, the poor devil, head, shoulders, and arms out of water all the time, screeching in a heart-rending way. He was carried along in this fashion for several hundred feet, when he was dragged beneath the surface.

I swam doggedly on, hoping that that was the last unattached shark. But there was another. Whether it was one that had attacked the natives earlier, or whether it was one that had made a good meal elsewhere, I do not know. At any rate, he was not in such haste as the others. I could not swim so rapidly now, for a large part of my effort was devoted to keeping track of him. I was watching him when he made his first attack. By good luck I got both hands on his nose, and, though his momentum nearly shoved me under, I managed to keep him off. He veered clear, and began circling about again. A second time I escaped him by the same manœuvre. The third rush was a miss on both sides. He sheered at the moment my hands should have landed on his nose, but his sandpaper hide (I had on a sleeveless undershirt) scraped the skin off one arm from elbow to shoulder.

By this time I was played out, and gave up hope. The schooner was still two hundred feet away. My face was in the water, and I was watching him manœuvre for another attempt, when I saw a brown body pass between us. It was Otoo.

"Swim for the schooner, master!" he said. And he spoke gayly, as though the affair was a mere lark. "I know sharks. The shark is my brother."

I obeyed, swimming slowly on, while Otoo swam about me, keeping always between me and the shark, foiling his rushes and encouraging me.

"The davit tackle carried away, and they are rigging the falls," he explained, a minute or so later, and then went under to head off another attack.

By the time the schooner was thirty feet away I was about done for. I could scarcely move. They were heaving lines at us from on board, but they continually fell short. The shark, finding that it was receiving no hurt, had become bolder. Several times it nearly got me, but each time Otoo was there just the moment before it was too late. Of course, Otoo could have saved himself any time. But he stuck by me.

"Good-by, Charley! I'm finished!" I just managed to gasp.

I knew that the end had come, and that the next moment I should throw up my hands and go down.

But Otoo laughed in my face, saying:

"I will show you a new trick. I will make that shark feel sick!"

He dropped in behind me, where the shark was preparing to come at me.

"A little more to the left!" he next called out. "There is a line there on the water. To the left, master—to the left!"

I changed my course and struck out blindly. I was by that time barely conscious. As my hand closed on the line I heard an exclamation from on board. I turned and looked. There was no sign of Otoo. The next instant he broke surface. Both hands were off at the wrist, the stumps spouting blood.

"Otoo!" he called softly. And I could see in his gaze the love that thrilled in his voice.

Then, and then only, at the very last of all our years, he called me by that name.

"Good-by, Otoo!" he called.

Then he was dragged under, and I was hauled aboard, where I fainted in the captain's arms.

And so passed Otoo, who saved me and made me a man, and who saved me in the end. We met in the maw of a hurricane, and parted in the maw of a shark, with seventeen intervening years of comradeship, the like of which I dare to assert has never befallen two men, the one brown and the other white. If Jehovah be from His high place watching every sparrow fall, not least in His kingdom shall be Otoo, the one heathen of Bora Bora.

The Terrible Solomons

There is no gainsaying that the Solomons are a hard-bitten bunch of islands. On the other hand, there are worse places in the world. But to the new chum who has no constitutional understanding of men and life in the rough, the Solomons may indeed prove terrible.

It is true that fever and dysentery are perpetually on the walkabout, that loathsome skin diseases abound, that the air is saturated with a poison that bites into every pore, cut, or abrasion and plants malignant ulcers, and that many strong men who escape dying there return as wrecks to their own countries. It is also true that the natives of the Solomons are a wild lot, with a hearty appetite for human flesh and a fad for collecting human heads. Their highest instinct of sportsmanship is to catch a man with his back turned and to smite him a cunning blow with a tomahawk that severs the spinal column at the base of the brain. It is equally true that on some islands, such as Malaita, the profit and loss account of social intercourse is calculated in homicides. Heads are a medium of exchange, and white heads are extremely valuable. Very often a dozen villages make a jackpot, which they fatten moon by moon, against the time when some brave warrior presents a white man's head, fresh and gory, and claims the pot.

All the foregoing is quite true, and yet there are white men who have lived in the Solomons a score of years and who feel homesick when they go away from them. A man needs only to be careful—and lucky—to live a long time in the Solomons; but he must also be of the right sort. He must have the hall-mark of the inevitable white man stamped upon his soul. He must be inevitable. He must have a certain grand carelessness of odds, a certain colossal self-satisfaction, and a racial egotism that convinces him that one white is better than a thousand niggers every day in the week, and that on Sunday he is able to clean out two thousand niggers. For such are the things that have made the white man inevitable. Oh, and one other thing—the white man who wishes to be inevitable, must not merely despise the lesser breeds and think a lot of himself; he must also fail to be too long on imagination. He must not understand too well the instincts, customs, and mental processes of the blacks, the yellows, and the browns; for it is not in such fashion that the white race has tramped its royal road around the world.

Bertie Arkwright was not inevitable. He was too sensitive, too finely strung, and he possessed too much imagination. The world was too much with him. He projected himself too quiveringly into his environment. Therefore, the last place in the world for him to come was the Solomons. He did not come, expecting to stay. A five weeks' stop-over between steamers, he decided, would satisfy the call of the primitive he felt thrumming the strings of his being. At least, so he told the lady tourists on the *Makembo*, though in different terms; and they worshipped him as a hero, for they were lady tourists and they would know only the safety of the steamer's deck as she threaded her way through the Solomons.

There was another man on board, of whom the ladies took no notice. He was a little shrivelled wisp of a man, with a withered skin the color of mahogany. His name on the passenger list does not matter, but his other name, Captain Malu, was a name for niggers to conjure with, and to scare naughty pickaninnies to righteousness, from New Hanover to the New Hebrides. He had farmed savages and savagery, and from fever and hardship, the crack of Sniders and the lash of the overseers, had wrested five millions of money in the form of bêche-de-mer, sandalwood, pearl-shell and turtle-shell, ivory-nuts and copra, grasslands, trading stations, and plantations. Captain Malu's little finger, which was broken, had more inevitableness in it than Bertie Arkwright's whole carcass. But then, the lady tourists had nothing by which to judge save appearances, and Bertie certainly was a fine-looking man.

Bertie talked with Captain Malu in the smoking-room, confiding to him his intention of seeing life red and bleeding in the Solomons. Captain Malu agreed that the intention was ambitious and honorable. It was not until several days later that he became interested in Bertie, when that young adventurer insisted on showing him an automatic 44-calibre pistol. Bertie explained the mechanism and demonstrated by slipping a loaded magazine up the hollow butt.

"It is so simple," he said. He shot the outer barrel back along the inner one. "That loads it and cocks it, you see. And then all I have to do is pull the trigger, eight times, as fast as I can quiver my finger. See that safety clutch. That's what I like about it. It is safe. It is positively fool-proof." He slipped out the magazine. "You see how safe it is."

As he held it in his hand, the muzzle came in line with Captain Malu's stomach. Captain Malu's blue eyes looked at it unswervingly.

"Would you mind pointing it in some other direction?" he asked.

"It's perfectly safe," Bertie assured him. "I withdrew the magazine. It's not loaded now, you know."

"A gun is always loaded."

"But this one isn't."

"Turn it away just the same."

Captain Malu's voice was flat and metallic and low, but his eyes never left the muzzle until the line of it was drawn past him and away from him.

"I'll bet a fiver it isn't loaded," Bertie proposed warmly.

The other shook his head.

"Then I'll show you."

Bertie started to put the muzzle to his own temple with the evident intention of pulling the trigger.

"Just a second," Captain Malu said quietly, reaching out his hand. "Let me look at it."

He pointed it seaward and pulled the trigger. A heavy explosion followed, instantaneous with the sharp click of the mechanism that flipped a hot and smoking cartridge sidewise along the deck. Bertie's jaw dropped in amazement.

"I slipped the barrel back once, didn't I?" he explained. "It was silly of me, I must say."

He giggled flabbily, and sat down in a steamer chair. The blood had ebbed from his face, exposing dark circles under his eyes. His hands were trembling and unable to guide the shaking cigarette to his lips. The world was too much with him, and he saw himself with dripping brains prone upon the deck.

"Really," he said, ". . . really."

"It's a pretty weapon," said Captain Malu, returning the automatic to him.

The Commissioner was on board the *Makembo,* returning from Sydney, and by his permission a stop was made at Ugi to land a missionary. And at Ugi lay the ketch *Arla,* Captain Hansen, skipper. Now the *Arla* was one of many vessels owned by Captain Malu, and it was at his suggestion and by his invitation that Bertie went aboard the *Arla* as guest for a four days' recruiting cruise on the coast of Malaita. Thereafter the *Arla* would drop him at Reminge Plantation (also owned by Captain Malu), where Bertie could remain for a week, and then be sent over to Tulagi, the seat of government, where he would become the Commissioner's guest. Captain Malu was responsible for two other suggestions, which given, he disappears from this narrative. One was to Captain Hansen, the other to Mr. Harriwell, manager of Reminge Plantation. Both suggestions were similar in tenor, namely, to give Mr. Bertram Arkwright an insight into the rawness and redness of life in the Solomons. Also, it is whispered that Captain Malu mentioned that a case of Scotch would be coincidental with any particularly gorgeous insight Mr. Arkwright might receive.

      o   o   o   o   o   o

"Yes, Swartz always was too pig-headed. You see, he took four of his boat's crew to Tulagi to be flogged—officially, you know—then started back with them in the whale-boat. It was pretty squally, and the boat capsized just outside. Swartz was the only one drowned. Of course it was an accident."

"Was it? Really?" Bertie asked, only half-interested, staring hard at the black man at the wheel.

Ugi had dropped astern, and the *Arla* was sliding along through a summer sea toward the wooded ranges of Malaita. The helmsman who so attracted Bertie's eyes sported a ten penny nail, stuck skewerwise through his nose. About his neck was a string of pants buttons. Thrust through holes in his ears were a can-opener, the broken handle of a tooth-brush, a clay pipe, the brass wheel of an alarm clock, and several Winchester rifle cartridges. On his chest, suspended from around his neck hung the half of a china plate. Some forty similarly apparelled blacks lay about the deck, fifteen of which were boat's crew, the remainder being fresh labor recruits.

"Of course it was an accident," spoke up the *Arla*'s mate, Jacobs, a slender, dark-eyed man who looked more a professor than a sailor. "Johnny Bedip nearly had the same kind of accident. He was bringing back several from a flogging, when they capsized him. But he knew how to swim as well as they, and two of them were drowned. He used a boat-stretcher and a revolver. Of course it was an accident."

"Quite common, them accidents," remarked the skipper. "You see that man at the wheel, Mr. Arkwright? He's a man-eater. Six months ago, he and the rest of the boat's crew drowned the then captain of the *Arla*. They did it on deck, sir, right aft there by the mizzen-traveller."

"The deck was in a shocking state," said the mate.

"Do I understand—?" Bertie began.

"Yes, just that," said Captain Hansen. "It was accidental drowning."

"But on deck—?"

"Just so. I don't mind telling you, in confidence, of course, that they used an axe."

"This present crew of yours?"

Captain Hansen nodded.

"The other skipper always was too careless," explained the mate. "He but just turned his back, when they let him have it."

"We haven't any show down here," was the skipper's complaint. "The government protects a nigger against a white every time. You can't shoot first. You've got to give the nigger first shot, or else the government calls it murder and you go to Fiji. That's why there's so many drowning accidents."

Dinner was called, and Bertie and the skipper went below, leaving the mate to watch on deck.

"Keep an eye out for that black devil, Auiki," was the skipper's parting caution. "I haven't liked his looks for several days."

"Right O," said the mate.

Dinner was part way along, and the skipper was in the middle of his story of the cutting out of the *Scottish Chiefs*.

"Yes," he was saying, "she was the finest vessel on the coast. But when she missed stays, and before ever she hit the reef, the canoes started for her. There were five white men, a crew of twenty Santa Cruz boys and Samoans, and only the supercargo escaped. Besides, there were sixty recruits. They were all *kai-kai'd*. *Kai-kai?*—oh, I beg your pardon. I mean they were eaten. Then there was the *James Edwards*, a dandy-rigged—"

But at that moment there was a sharp oath from the mate on deck and a chorus of savage cries. A revolver went off three times, and then was heard a loud splash. Captain Hansen had sprung up the companionway on the instant, and Bertie's eyes had been fascinated by a glimpse of him drawing his revolver as he sprang. Bertie went up more circumspectly, hesitating before he put his head above the companionway slide. But nothing happened. The mate was shaking with excitement, his revolver in his hand. Once he startled, and half-jumped around, as if danger threatened his back.

"One of the natives fell overboard," he was saying, in a queer tense voice. "He couldn't swim."

"Who was it?" the skipper demanded.

"Auiki," was the answer.

"But I say, you know, I heard shots," Bertie said, in trembling eagerness, for he scented adventure, and adventure that was happily over with.

The mate whirled upon him, snarling:

"It's a damned lie. There ain't been a shot fired. The nigger fell overboard."

Captain Hansen regarded Bertie with unblinking, lack-lustre eyes.

"I—I thought—" Bertie was beginning.

"Shots?" said Captain Hansen, dreamily. "Shots? Did you hear any shots, Mr. Jacobs?"

"Not a shot," replied Mr. Jacobs.

The skipper looked at his guest triumphantly, and said:

"Evidently an accident. Let us go down, Mr. Arkwright, and finish dinner."

Bertie slept that night in the captain's cabin, a tiny state-room off the main-cabin. The for'ard bulkhead was decorated with a stand of rifles. Over the bunk were three more rifles. Under the bunk was a big drawer, which, when he pulled it out, he found filled with ammunition, dynamite, and several boxes of detonators. He elected to take the settee on the opposite side. Lying conspicuously on the small table, was the *Arla*'s log. Bertie did not know that it had been especially prepared for the occasion by Captain Malu, and he read therein how on September 21, two boat's crew had fallen overboard and been drowned. Bertie read between the lines and knew better. He read how the *Arla*'s whale-boat had been bushwhacked at Su'u and had lost three men; of how the skipper discovered the cook stewing human flesh on the galley fire—flesh purchased by the boat's crew ashore in Fui; of how an accidental discharge of dynamite, while signalling, had killed another boat's crew; of night attacks; ports fled from between the dawns; attacks by bushmen in mangrove swamps and by fleets of salt-water men in the larger passages. One item that occurred with monotonous frequency was death by dysentery. He noticed with alarm that two white men had so died—guests, like himself, on the *Arla*.

"I say, you know," Bertie said next day to Captain Hansen. "I've been glancing through your log."

The skipper displayed quick vexation that the log had been left lying about.

"And all that dysentery, you know, that's all rot, just like the accidental drownings," Bertie continued. "What does dysentery really stand for?"

The skipper openly admired his guest's acumen, stiffened himself to make indignant denial, then gracefully surrendered. "You see, it's like this, Mr. Arkwright. These islands have got a bad enough name as it is. It's getting harder every day to sign on white men. Suppose a man is killed. The company has to pay through the nose for another man to take the job. But if the man merely dies of sickness, it's all right. The new chums don't mind disease. What they draw the line at is being murdered. I thought the skipper of the *Arla* had died of dysentery when I took his billet. Then it was too late. I'd signed the contract."

"Besides," said Mr. Jacobs, "there's altogether too many accidental drownings anyway. It don't look right. It's the fault of the government. A white man hasn't a chance to defend himself from the niggers."

"Yes, look at the *Princess* and that Yankee mate," the skipper took up the tale. "She carried five white men besides a government agent. The captain, the agent, and the supercargo were ashore in the two boats. They were killed to the last man. The mate and boson, with about fifteen of the crew—Samoans and Tongans—were on board. A crowd of niggers came off from shore. First thing the mate knew, the boson and the crew were killed in the first rush. The mate grabbed three cartridge-belts and two Winchesters and skinned up to the cross-trees. He was the sole survivor, and you can't blame him for being mad. He pumped one rifle till it got so hot he couldn't hold it, then he pumped the other. The deck was black with niggers. He cleaned them out. He dropped them as they went over the rail, and he dropped them as fast as they picked up their paddles. Then they jumped into the water and started to swim for it, and, being mad, he got half a dozen more. And what did he get for it?"

"Seven years in Fiji," snapped the mate.

"The government said he wasn't justified in shooting after they'd taken to the water," the skipper explained.

"And that's why they die of dysentery nowadays," the mate added.

"Just fancy," said Bertie, as he felt a longing for the cruise to be over.

Later on in the day he interviewed the black who had been

pointed out to him as a cannibal. This fellow's name was
Sumasai. He had spent three years on a Queensland plantation.
He had been to Samoa, and Fiji, and Sydney; and as a boat's
crew had been on recruiting schooners through New Britain,
New Ireland, New Guinea, and the Admiralties. Also, he was a
wag, and he had taken a line on his skipper's conduct. Yes, he
had eaten many men. How many? He could not remember the
tally. Yes, white men, too; they were very good, unless they were
sick. He had once eaten a sick one.

"My word!" he cried, at the recollection. "Me sick plenty
along him. My belly walk about too much."

Bertie shuddered, and asked about heads. Yes, Sumasai had
several hidden ashore, in good condition, sun-dried, and smoke-
cured. One was of the captain of a schooner. It had long
whiskers. He would sell it for two quid. Black men's heads he
would sell for one quid. He had some pickaninny heads, in poor
condition, that he would let go for ten bob.

Five minutes afterward, Bertie found himself sitting on the
companionway-slide alongside a black with a horrible skin disease. He sheered off, and on inquiry was told that it was leprosy.
He hurried below and washed himself with antiseptic soap. He
took many antiseptic washes in the course of the day, for every
native on board was afflicted with malignant ulcers of one sort
or another.

As the *Arla* drew in to an anchorage in the midst of mangrove
swamps, a double row of barbed wire was stretched around
above her rail. That looked like business, and when Bertie saw
the shore canoes alongside, armed with spears, bows and
arrows, and Sniders, he wished more earnestly than ever that
the cruise was over.

That evening the natives were slow in leaving the ship at sundown. A number of them checked the mate when he ordered
them ashore.

"Never mind, I'll fix them," said Captain Hansen, diving
below.

When he came back, he showed Bertie a stick of dynamite
attached to a fish-hook. Now it happens that a paper-wrapped
bottle of chlorodyne with a piece of harmless fuse projecting can

fool anybody. It fooled Bertie, and it fooled the natives. When Captain Hansen lighted the fuse and hooked the fish-hook into the tail-end of a native's loin-cloth, that native was smitten with so ardent a desire for the shore that he forgot to shed the loin-cloth. He started for'ard, the fuse sizzling and spluttering at his rear, the natives in his path taking headers over the barbed wire at every jump. Bertie was horror-stricken. So was Captain Hansen. He had forgotten his twenty-five recruits, on each of which he had paid thirty shillings advance. They went over the side along with the shore-dwelling folk and followed by him who trailed the sizzling chlorodyne bottle.

Bertie did not see the bottle go off; but the mate opportunely discharging a stick of real dynamite aft where it would harm nobody, Bertie would have sworn in any admiralty court to a nigger blown to flinders.

The flight of the twenty-five recruits had actually cost the *Arla* forty pounds, and, since they had taken to the bush, there was no hope of recovering them. The skipper and his mate proceeded to drown their sorrow in cold tea. The cold tea was in whiskey bottles, so Bertie did not know it was cold tea they were mopping up. All he knew was that the two men got very drunk and argued eloquently and at length as to whether the exploded nigger should be reported as a case of dysentery or as an accidental drowning. When they snored off to sleep, he was the only white man left, and he kept a perilous watch till dawn, in fear of an attack from shore and an uprising of the crew.

Three more days the *Arla* spent on the coast, and three more nights the skipper and the mate drank overfondly of cold tea, leaving Bertie to keep the watch. They knew he could be depended upon, while he was equally certain that if he lived, he would report their drunken conduct to Captain Malu. Then the *Arla* dropped anchor at Reminge Plantation, on Guadalcanar, and Bertie landed on the beach with a sigh of relief and shook hands with the manager. Mr. Harriwell was ready for him.

"Now you mustn't be alarmed if some of our fellows seem downcast," Mr. Harriwell said, having drawn him aside in confidence. "There's been talk of an outbreak, and two or three sus-

picious signs I'm willing to admit, but personally I think it's all
poppycock."

"How—how many blacks have you on the plantation?" Bertie
asked, with a sinking heart.

"We're working four hundred just now," replied Mr.
Harriwell, cheerfully; "but the three of us, with you, of course,
and the skipper and mate of the *Arla,* can handle them all right."

Bertie turned to meet one McTavish, the storekeeper, who
scarcely acknowledged the introduction, such was his eagerness
to present his resignation.

"It being that I'm a married man, Mr. Harriwell, I can't very
well afford to remain on longer. Trouble is working up, as plain
as the nose on your face. The niggers are going to break out, and
there'll be another Hohono horror here."

"What's a Hohono horror?" Bertie asked, after the storekeeper
had been persuaded to remain until the end of the month.

"Oh, he means Hohono Plantation, on Ysabel," said the manager. "The niggers killed the five white men ashore, captured
the schooner, killed the captain and mate, and escaped in a body
to Malaita. But I always said they were careless on Hohono.
They won't catch us napping here. Come along, Mr. Arkwright,
and see our view from the veranda."

Bertie was too busy wondering how he could get away to
Tulagi to the Commissioner's house, to see much of the view. He
was still wondering, when a rifle exploded very near to him,
behind his back. At the same moment his arm was nearly dislocated, so eagerly did Mr. Harriwell drag him indoors.

"I say, old man, that was a close shave," said the manager,
pawing him over to see if he had been hit. "I can't tell you how
sorry I am. But it was broad daylight, and I never dreamed."

Bertie was beginning to turn pale.

"They got the other manager that way," McTavish vouchsafed.
"And a dashed fine chap he was. Blew his brains out all over the
veranda. You noticed that dark stain there between the steps
and the door?"

Bertie was ripe for the cocktail which Mr. Harriwell pitched
in and compounded for him; but before he could drink it, a man
in riding trousers and puttees entered.

"What's the matter now?" the manager asked, after one look at the newcomer's face. "Is the river up again?"

"River be blowed—it's the niggers. Stepped out of the cane-grass, not a dozen feet away, and whopped at me. It was a Snider, and he shot from the hip. Now what I want to know is where'd he get that Snider?—Oh, I beg pardon. Glad to know you, Mr. Arkwright."

"Mr. Brown is my assistant," explained Mr. Harriwell. "And now let's have that drink."

"But where'd he get that Snider?" Mr. Brown insisted. "I always objected to keeping those guns on the premises."

"They're still there," Mr. Harriwell said, with a show of heat.

Mr. Brown smiled incredulously.

"Come along and see," said the manager.

Bertie joined the procession into the office, where Mr. Harriwell pointed triumphantly at a big packing-case in a dusty corner.

"Well, then, where did the beggar get that Snider?" harped Mr. Brown.

But just then McTavish lifted the packing-case. The manager started, then tore off the lid. The case was empty. They gazed at one another in horrified silence. Harriwell drooped wearily.

Then McVeigh cursed.

"What I contended all along—the house-boys are not to be trusted."

"It does look serious," Harriwell admitted, "but we'll come through it all right. What the sanguinary niggers need is a shaking up. Will you gentlemen please bring your rifles to dinner, and will you, Mr. Brown, kindly prepare forty or fifty sticks of dynamite. Make the fuses good and short. We'll give them a lesson. And now, gentlemen, dinner is served."

One thing that Bertie detested was rice and curry, so it happened that he alone partook of an inviting omelet. He had quite finished his plate, when Harriwell helped himself to the omelet. One mouthful he tasted, then spat out vociferously.

"That's the second time," McTavish announced ominously.

Harriwell was still hawking and spitting.

"Second time, what?" Bertie quavered.

"Poison," was the answer. "That cook will be hanged yet."

"That's the way the bookkeeper went out at Cape Marsh," Brown spoke up. "Died horribly. They said on the *Jessie* that they heard him screaming three miles away."

"I'll put the cook in irons," sputtered Harriwell. "Fortunately we discovered it in time."

Bertie sat paralysed. There was no color in his face. He attempted to speak, but only an inarticulate gurgle resulted. All eyed him anxiously.

"Don't say it, don't say it," McTavish cried in a tense voice.

"Yes, I ate it, plenty of it, a whole plateful!" Bertie cried explosively, like a diver suddenly regaining breath.

The awful silence continued half a minute longer, and he read his fate in their eyes.

"Maybe it wasn't poison after all," said Harriwell, dismally.

"Call in the cook," said Brown.

In came the cook, a grinning black boy, nose-spiked and ear-plugged.

"Here, you, Wi-wi, what name that?" Harriwell bellowed, pointing accusingly at the omelet.

Wi-wi was very naturally frightened and embarrassed.

"Him good fella *kai-kai*," he murmured apologetically.

"Make him eat it," suggested McTavish. "That's a proper test."

Harriwell filled a spoon with the stuff and jumped for the cook, who fled in panic.

"That settles it," was Brown's solemn pronouncement. "He won't eat it."

"Mr. Brown, will you please go and put the irons on him?" Harriwell turned cheerfully to Bertie. "It's all right, old man, the Commissioner will deal with him, and if you die, depend upon it, he will be hanged."

"Don't think the government'll do it," objected McTavish.

"But gentlemen, gentlemen," Bertie cried. "In the meantime think of me."

Harriwell shrugged his shoulders pityingly.

"Sorry, old man, but it's a native poison, and there are no known antidotes for native poisons. Try and compose yourself, and if—"

Two sharp reports of a rifle from without, interrupted the dis-
course, and Brown, entering, reloaded his rifle and sat down to
table.

"The cook's dead," he said. "Fever. A rather sudden attack."

"I was just telling Mr. Arkwright that there are no antidotes
for native poison—"

"Except gin," said Brown.

Harriwell called himself an absent-minded idiot and rushed
for the gin bottle.

"Neat, man, neat," he warned Bertie, who gulped down a
tumbler two-thirds full of the raw spirits, and coughed and
choked from the angry bite of it till the tears ran down his
cheeks.

Harriwell took his pulse and temperature, made a show of
looking out for him, and doubted that the omelet had been poi-
soned. Brown and McTavish also doubted; but Bertie discerned
an insincere ring in their voices. His appetite had left him, and
he took his own pulse stealthily under the table. There was no
question but what it was increasing, but he failed to ascribe it to
the gin he had taken. McTavish, rifle in hand, went out on the
veranda to reconnoitre.

"They're massing up at the cook-house," was his report. "And
they've no end of Sniders. My idea is to sneak around on the
other side and take them in flank. Strike the first blow, you
know. Will you come along, Brown?"

Harriwell ate on steadily, while Bertie discovered that his
pulse had leaped up five beats. Nevertheless, he could not help
jumping when the rifles began to go off. Above the scattering of
Sniders could be heard the pumping of Brown's and McTavish's
Winchesters—all against a background of demoniacal screeching and yelling.

"They've got them on the run," Harriwell remarked, as
voices and gunshots faded away in the distance.

Scarcely were Brown and McTavish back at the table when
the latter reconnoitred.

"They've got dynamite," he said.

"Then let's charge them with dynamite," Harriwell proposed.

Thrusting half a dozen sticks each into their pockets and

equipping themselves with lighted cigars, they started for the door. And just then it happened. They blamed McTavish for it afterward, and he admitted that the charge had been a trifle excessive. But at any rate it went off under the house, which lifted up cornerwise and settled back on its foundations. Half the china on the table was shattered, while the eight-day clock stopped. Yelling for vengeance, the three men rushed out into the night, and the bombardment began.

When they returned, there was no Bertie. He had dragged himself away to the office, barricaded himself in, and sunk upon the floor in a gin-soaked nightmare, wherein he died a thousand deaths while the valorous fight went on around him. In the morning, sick and headachey from the gin, he crawled out to find the sun still in the sky and God presumably in heaven, for his hosts were alive and uninjured.

Harriwell pressed him to stay on longer, but Bertie insisted on sailing immediately on the *Arla* for Tulagi, where, until the following steamer day, he stuck close by the Commissioner's house. There were lady tourists on the outgoing steamer, and Bertie was again a hero, while Captain Malu, as usual, passed unnoticed. But Captain Malu sent back from Sydney two cases of the best Scotch whiskey on the market, for he was not able to make up his mind as to whether it was Captain Hansen or Mr. Harriwell who had given Bertie Arkwright the more gorgeous insight into life in the Solomons.

The Inevitable White Man

"The black will never understand the white, nor the white the black, as long as black is black and white is white."

So said Captain Woodward. We sat in the parlor of Charley Roberts' pub in Apia, drinking long Abu Hameds compounded and shared with us by the aforesaid Charley Roberts, who claimed the recipe direct from Stevens, famous for having invented the Abu Hamed at a time when he was spurred on by Nile thirst—the Stevens who was responsible for "With Kitchener to Kartoun," and who passed out at the siege of Ladysmith.

Captain Woodward, short and squat, elderly, burned by forty years of tropic sun, and with the most beautiful liquid brown eyes I ever saw in a man, spoke from a vast experience. The crisscross of scars on his bald pate bespoke a tomahawk intimacy with the black, and of equal intimacy was the advertisement, front and rear, on the right side of his neck, where an arrow had at one time entered and been pulled clean through. As he explained, he had been in a hurry on that occasion—the arrow impeded his running—and he felt that he could not take the time to break off the head and pull out the shaft the way it had come in. At the present moment he was commander of the *Savaii*, the big steamer that recruited labor from the westward for the German plantations on Samoa.

"Half the trouble is the stupidity of the whites," said Roberts, pausing to take a swig from his glass and to curse the Samoan bar-boy in affectionate terms. "If the white man would lay himself out a bit to understand the workings of the black man's mind, most of the messes would be avoided."

"I've seen a few who claimed they understood niggers," Captain Woodward retorted, "and I always took notice that they were the first to be *kai-kai'd* (eaten). Look at the missionaries in New Guinea and the New Hebrides—the martyr isle of Erromanga and all the rest. Look at the Austrian expedition that was cut to pieces in the Solomons, in the bush of Gaudalcanar. And look at the traders themselves, with a score of years' experience, making their brag that no nigger would ever get them, and whose heads to this day are ornamenting the rafters of the canoe houses. There was old Johnny Simons—twenty-six years on the raw edges of Melanesia, swore he knew the niggers like a book and that they'd never do for him, and he passed out at Marovo Lagoon, New Georgia, had his head sawed off by a black Mary (woman) and an old nigger with only one leg, having left the other leg in the mouth of a shark while diving for dynamited fish. There was Billy Watts, horrible reputation as a nigger killer, a man to scare the devil. I remember lying at Cape Little, New Ireland you know, when the niggers stole half a case of trade-tobacco—cost him about three dollars and a half. In retaliation he turned out, shot six niggers, smashed up their war canoes and burned two villages. And it was at Cape Little, four years afterward, that he was jumped along with fifty Buku boys he had with him fishing bêche-de-mer. In five minutes they were all dead, with the exception of three boys who got away in a canoe. Don't talk to me about understanding the nigger. The white man's mission is to farm the world, and it's a big enough job cut out for him. What time has he got left to understand niggers anyway?"

"Just so," said Roberts. "And somehow it doesn't seem necessary, after all, to understand the niggers. In direct proportion to the white man's stupidity is his success in farming the world—"

"And putting the fear of God into the nigger's heart," Captain Woodward blurted out. "Perhaps you're right, Roberts. Perhaps it's his stupidity that makes him succeed, and surely one phase of his stupidity is his inability to understand the niggers. But there's one thing sure, the white has to run the niggers whether he understands them or not. It's inevitable. It's fate."

"And of course the white man is inevitable—it's the niggers' fate," Roberts broke in. "Tell the white man there's pearl-shell in some lagoon infested by ten thousand howling cannibals, and he'll head there all by his lonely, with half a dozen kanaka divers and a tin alarm clock for chronometer, all packed like sardines on a commodious, five-ton ketch. Whisper that there's a gold strike at the North Pole, and that same inevitable white-skinned creature will set out at once, armed with pick and shovel, a side of bacon, and the latest patent rocker—and what's more, he'll get there. Tip it off to him that there's diamonds on the red-hot ramparts of hell, and Mr. White Man will storm the ramparts and set old Satan himself to pick-and-shovel work. That's what comes of being stupid and inevitable."

"But I wonder what the black man must think of the—the inevitableness," I said.

Captain Woodward broke into quiet laughter. His eyes had a reminiscent gleam.

"I'm just wondering what the niggers of Malu thought and still must be thinking of the one inevitable white man we had on board when we visited them in the *Duchess*," he explained.

Roberts mixed three more Abu Hameds.

"That was twenty years ago. Saxtorph was his name. He was certainly the most stupid man I ever saw, but he was as inevitable as death. There was only one thing that chap could do, and that was shoot. I remember the first time I ran into him—right here in Apia, twenty years ago. That was before your time, Roberts. I was sleeping at Dutch Henry's hotel, down where the market is now. Ever heard of him? He made a tidy stake smuggling arms in to the rebels, sold out his hotel, and was killed in Sydney just six weeks afterward in a saloon row.

"But Saxtorph. One night I'd just got to sleep, when a couple of cats began to sing in the courtyard. It was out of bed and up window, water jug in hand. But just then I heard the window of the next room go up. Two shots were fired, and the window was closed. I fail to impress you with the celerity of the transaction. Ten seconds at the outside. Up went the window, bang bang went the revolver, and down went the window. Whoever it was, he had never stopped to see the effect of his shots. He knew. Do you follow me?—he *knew*. There was no more cat-concert, and in the morning there lay the two offenders, stone-dead. It was marvellous to me. It still is marvellous. First, it was starlight, and Saxtorph shot without drawing a bead; next, he shot so rapidly that the two reports were like a double report; and finally, he knew he had hit his marks without looking to see.

"Two days afterward he came on board to see me. I was mate, then, on the *Duchess*, a whacking big one-hundred-and-fifty-ton schooner, a blackbirder. And let me tell you that blackbirders were blackbirders in those days. There weren't any government inspectors, and no government protection for *us*, either. It was rough work, give and take, if we were finished, and nothing said, and we ran niggers from every south sea island they didn't kick us off from. Well, Saxtorph came on board, John Saxtorph was the name he gave. He was a sandy little man, hair sandy, complexion sandy, and eyes sandy, too. Nothing striking about him. His soul was as neutral as his color scheme. He said he was strapped and wanted to ship on board. Would go cabin-boy, cook, supercargo, or common sailor. Didn't know anything about any of the billets, but said that he was willing to learn. I didn't want him, but his shooting had so impressed me that I took him as common sailor, wages three pounds per month.

"He was willing to learn all right, I'll say that much. But he was constitutionally unable to learn anything. He could no more box the compass than I could mix drinks like Roberts here. And as for steering, he gave me my first gray hairs. I never dared risk him at the wheel when we were running in a big sea, while full-and-by and close-and-by were insoluble mysteries. Couldn't ever tell the difference between a sheet and a tackle, simply couldn't. The fore-throat-jig and the jib-jig were all one to him. Tell him to slack off the mainsheet, and before you know it, he'd drop the peak. He fell overboard three times, and he couldn't swim. But he was always cheerful, never seasick, and he was the most willing man I ever knew. He was an uncommunicative soul. Never talked about himself. His history, so far as we were concerned, began the day he signed on the *Duchess*. Where he learned to shoot, the stars alone can tell. He was a Yankee—that much we knew from the twang in his speech. And that was all we ever did know.

"And now we begin to get to the point. We had bad luck in the New Hebrides, only fourteen boys for five weeks, and we ran up before the southeast for the Solomons. Malaita, then as now, was good recruiting ground, and we ran into Malu, on the northwestern corner. There's a shore reef and an outer reef, and a mighty nervous anchorage; but we made it all right and fired off our dynamite as a signal to the niggers to come down and be recruited. In three days we got not a boy. The niggers came off to us in their canoes by hundreds, but they only laughed when we showed them beads and calico and hatchets and talked of the delights of plantation work in Samoa.

"On the fourth day there came a change. Fifty-odd boys signed on and were billeted in the main-hold, with the freedom of the deck, of course. And of course, looking back, this whole-sale signing on was suspicious, but at the time we thought some powerful chief had removed the ban against recruiting. The morning of the fifth day our two boats went ashore as usual— one to cover the other, you know, in case of trouble. And, as usual, the fifty niggers on board were on deck, loafing, talking, smoking, and sleeping. Saxtorph and myself, along with four other sailors, were all that were left on board. The two boats were manned with Gilbert Islanders. In the one were the captain, the supercargo, and the recruiter. In the other, which was the covering boat and which lay off shore a hundred yards, was the second mate. Both boats were well-armed, though trouble was little expected.

"Four of the sailors, including Saxtorph, were scraping the poop rail. The fifth sailor, rifle in hand, was standing guard by the water-tank just for'ard of the mainmast. I was for'ard, putting in the finishing licks on a new jaw for the fore-gaff. I was just reaching for my pipe where I had laid it down, when I heard a shot from shore. I straightened up to look. Something struck me on the back of the head, partially stunning me and knocking me to the deck. My first thought was that something had carried away aloft; but even as I went down, and before I struck the deck, I heard the devil's own tattoo of rifles from the boats, and, twisting sidewise, I caught a glimpse of the sailor who was standing guard. Two big niggers were holding his arms, and a third nigger, from behind, was braining him with a tomahawk.

"I can see it now, the water-tank, the mainmast, the gang hanging on to him, the hatchet descending on the back of his head, and all under the blazing sunlight. I was fascinated by that growing vision of death. The tomahawk seemed to take a horribly long time to come down. I saw it land, and the man's legs give under him as he crumpled. The niggers held him up by sheer strength while he was hacked a couple of times more. Then I got two more hacks on the head and decided that I was dead. So did the brute that was hacking me. I was too helpless to move, and I lay there and watched them removing the sentry's head. I must say they did it slick enough. They were old hands at the business.

"The riflefiring from the boats had ceased, and I made no doubt that they were finished off and that the end had come to everything. It was only a matter of moments when they would return for my head. They were evidently taking the heads from the sailors aft. Heads are valuable on Malaita, especially white heads. They have the place of honor in the canoe houses of the saltwater natives. What particular decorative effect the bushmen get out of them I didn't know, but they prize them just as much as the saltwater crowd.

"I had a dim notion of escaping, and I crawled on hands and knees to the winch, where I managed to drag myself to my feet. From there I could look aft and see three heads on top the cabin—the heads of three sailors I had given orders to for months. The niggers saw me standing, and started for me. I reached for my revolver, and found they had taken it. I can't say that I was scared. I've been near to death several times, but it never seemed easier than right then. I was half-stunned, and nothing seemed to matter.

"The leading nigger had armed himself with a cleaver from the galley, and he grimaced like an ape as he prepared to slice me down. But the slice was never made. He went down on the deck all of a heap, and I saw the blood gush from his mouth. In a dim way I heard a rifle go off and continue to go off. Nigger after nigger went down. My senses began to clear, and I noted

that there was never a miss. Every time that rifle went off a nigger dropped. I sat down on deck beside the winch and looked
up. Perched in the crosstrees was Saxtorph. How he had managed it I can't imagine, for he had carried up with him two
Winchesters and I don't know how many bandoliers of ammunition; and he was now doing the one only thing in this world
that he was fitted to do.

"I've seen shooting and slaughter, but I never saw anything
like that. I sat by the winch and watched the show. I was weak
and faint, and it seemed to be all a dream. Bang, bang, bang,
bang, went his rifle, and thud, thud, thud, thud, went the niggers to the deck. It was amazing to see them go down. After
their first rush to get me, when about a dozen had dropped,
they seemed paralysed; but he never left off pumping his gun.
By this time canoes and the two boats arrived from shore,
armed with Sniders, and with Winchesters which they had captured in the boats. The fusillade they let loose on Saxtorph was
tremendous. Luckily for him the niggers are only good at close
range. They are not used to putting the guns to their shoulders.
They wait until they are right on top of a man, and then they
shoot from the hip. When his rifle got too hot, Saxtorph
changed off. That had been his idea when he carried two rifles
up with him.

"The astounding thing was the rapidity of his fire. Also, he
never made a miss. If ever anything was inevitable, that man
was. It was the swiftness of it that made the slaughter so
appalling. The niggers did not have time to think. When they
did manage to think, they went over the side in a rush, capsiz-
ing the canoes of course. Saxtorph never let up. The water was
covered with them, and plump, plump, plump, he dropped his
bullets into them. Not a single miss, and I could hear distinctly
the thud of every bullet as it buried in human flesh.

"The niggers spread out and headed for the shore, swimming.
The water was carpeted with bobbing heads, and I stood up, as
in a dream, and watched it all—the bobbing heads and the
heads that ceased to bob. Some of the long shots were magnificent. Only one man reached the beach, but as he stood up to
wade ashore, Saxtorph got him. It was beautiful. And when a

couple of niggers ran down to drag him out of the water, Saxtorph got them, too.

"I thought everything was over then, when I heard the rifle go off again. A nigger had come out of the cabin companion on the run for the rail and gone down in the middle of it. The cabin must have been full of them. I counted twenty. They came up one at a time and jumped for the rail. But they never got there. It reminded me of trapshooting. A black body would pop out of the companion, bang would go Saxtorph's rifle, and down would go the black body. Of course, those below did not know what was happening on deck, so they continued to pop out until the last one was finished off.

"Saxtorph waited a while to make sure, and then came down on deck. He and I were all that were left of the *Duchess's* complement, and I was pretty well to the bad, while he was helpless now that the shooting was over. Under my direction he washed out my scalp-wounds and sewed them up. A big drink of whiskey braced me to make an effort to get out. There was nothing else to do. All the rest were dead. We tried to get up sail, Saxtorph hoisting and I holding the turn. He was once more the stupid lubber. He couldn't hoist worth a cent, and when I fell in a faint, it looked all up with us.

"When I came to, Saxtorph was sitting helplessly on the rail, waiting to ask me what he should do. I told him to overhaul the wounded and see if there were any able to crawl. He gathered together six. One, I remember, had a broken leg; but Saxtorph said his arms were all right. I lay in the shade, brushing the flies off and directing operations, while Saxtorph bossed his hospital gang. I'll be blessed if he didn't make those poor niggers heave at every rope on the pin-rails before he found the halyards. One of them let go the rope in the midst of the hoisting and slipped down to the deck dead; but Saxtorph hammered the others and made them stick by the job. When the fore and main were up, I told him to knock the shackle out of the anchor chain and let her go. I had had myself helped aft to the wheel, where I was going to make a shift at steering. I can't guess how he did it, but instead of knocking the shackle out, down went the second anchor, and there we were doubly moored.

"In the end he managed to knock both shackles out and raise the staysail and jib, and the *Duchess* filled away for the entrance. Our decks were a spectacle. Dead and dying niggers were everywhere. They were wedged away some of them in the most inconceivable places. The cabin was full of them where they had crawled off the deck and cashed in. I put Saxtorph and his graveyard gang to work heaving them overside, and over they went, the living and the dead. The sharks had fat pickings that day. Of course our four murdered sailors went the same way. Their heads, however, we put in a sack with weights, so that by no chance should they drift on the beach and fall into the hands of the niggers.

"Our five prisoners I decided to use as crew, but they decided otherwise. They watched their opportunity and went over the side. Saxtorph got two in mid-air with his revolver, and would have shot the other three in the water if I hadn't stopped him. I was sick of the slaughter, you see, and, besides, they'd helped work the schooner out. But it was mercy thrown away, for the sharks got the three of them.

"I had brain fever or something after we got clear of the land. Anyway, the *Duchess* lay hove to for three weeks, when I pulled myself together and we jogged on with her to Sydney. Anyway those niggers of Malu learned the everlasting lesson that it is not good to monkey with a white man. In their case, Saxtorph was certainly inevitable."

Charley Roberts emitted a long whistle and said:

"Well I should say so. But whatever became of Saxtorph?"

"He drifted into seal hunting and became a crackerjack. For six years he was high line of both the Victoria and San Francisco fleets. The seventh year his schooner was seized in Bering Sea by a Russian cruiser, and all hands, so the talk went, were slammed into the Siberian salt mines. At least I've never heard of him since."

"Farming the world," Roberts muttered. "Farming the world. Well here's to them. Somebody's got to do it—farm the world, I mean."

Captain Woodward rubbed the criss-crosses on his bald head.

"I've done my share of it," he said. "Forty years now. This will be my last trip. Then I'm going home to stay."

"I'll wager the wine you don't," Roberts challenged. "You'll die in the harness, not at home."

Captain Woodward promptly accepted the bet, but personally I think Charley Roberts has the best of it.

The Seed of McCoy

The *Pyrenees*, her iron sides pressed low in the water by her cargo of wheat, rolled sluggishly, and made it easy for the man who was climbing aboard from out a tiny outrigger canoe. As his eyes came level with the rail, so that he could see inboard, it seemed to him that he saw a dim, almost indiscernible haze. It was more like an illusion, like a blurring film that had spread abruptly over his eyes. He felt an inclination to brush it away, and the same instant he thought that he was growing old and that it was time to send to San Francisco for a pair of spectacles.

As he came over the rail he cast a glance aloft at the tall masts, and, next, at the pumps. They were not working. There seemed nothing the matter with the big ship, and he wondered why she had hoisted the signal of distress. He thought of his happy islanders, and hoped it was not disease. Perhaps the ship was short of water or provisions. He shook hands with the captain whose gaunt face and care-worn eyes made no secret of the trouble, whatever it was. At the same moment the new-comer was aware of a faint, indefinable smell. It seemed like that of burnt bread, but different.

He glanced curiously about him. Twenty feet away a weary-faced sailor was calking the deck. As his eye lingered on the man, he saw suddenly arise from under his hands a faint spiral of haze that curled and twisted and was gone. By now he had reached the deck. His bare feet were pervaded by a dull warmth that quickly penetrated the thick calluses. He knew now the nature of the ship's distress. His eyes roved swiftly forward, where the full crew of weary-faced sailors regarded him eagerly. The glance from his liquid brown eyes swept over them like a benediction, soothing them, wrapping them about as in the mantle of a great peace. "How long has she been afire, Captain?" he asked in a voice so gentle and unperturbed that it was as the cooing of a dove.

At first the captain felt the peace and content of it stealing in upon him; then the consciousness of all that he had gone through and was going through smote him, and he was resentful. By what right did this ragged beach-comber, in dungaree trousers and a cotton shirt, suggest such a thing as peace and content to him and his overwrought, exhausted soul? The captain did not reason this; it was the unconscious process of emotion that caused his resentment.

"Fifteen days," he answered shortly. "Who are you?"

"My name is McCoy," came the answer in tones that breathed tenderness and compassion.

"I mean, are you the pilot?"

McCoy passed the benediction of his gaze over the tall, heavy-shouldered man with the haggard, unshaven face who had joined the captain.

"I am as much a pilot as anybody," was McCoy's answer. "We are all pilots here, Captain, and I know every inch of these waters."

But the captain was impatient.

"What I want is some of the authorities. I want to talk with them, and blame quick."

"Then I'll do just as well."

Again that insidious suggestion of peace, and his ship a raging furnace beneath his feet! The captain's eyebrows lifted impatiently and nervously, and his fist clenched as if he were about to strike a blow with it.

"Who in hell are you?" he demanded.

"I am the chief magistrate," was the reply in a voice that was still the softest and gentlest imaginable.

The tall, heavy-shouldered man broke out in a harsh laugh that was partly amusement, but mostly hysterical. Both he and the captain regarded McCoy with incredulity and amazement. That this barefooted beach-comber should possess such high-sounding dignity was inconceivable. His cotton shirt, unbuttoned, exposed a grizzled chest and the fact that there was no undershirt beneath. A worn straw hat failed to hide the ragged gray hair. Halfway down his chest descended an untrimmed patriarchal beard. In any slop-slop, two shillings would have outfitted him complete as he stood before them.

"Any relation to the McCoy of the *Bounty*?" the captain asked.

"He was my great-grandfather."

"Oh," the captain said, then bethought himself. "My name is Davenport, and this is my first mate, Mr. Konig."

They shook hands.

"And now to business." The captain spoke quickly, the urgency of a great haste pressing his speech. "We've been on fire for over two weeks. She's ready to break all hell loose any moment. That's why I held for Pitcairn. I want to beach her, or scuttle her, and save the hull."

"Then you made a mistake, Captain," said McCoy. "You should have slacked away for Mangareva. There's a beautiful beach there, in a lagoon where the water is like a mill-pond."

"But we're here, ain't we?" the first mate demanded. "That's the point. We're here, and we've got to do something."

McCoy shook his head kindly.

"You can do nothing here. There is no beach. There isn't even anchorage."

"Gammon!" said the mate. "Gammon!" he repeated loudly, as the captain signalled him to be more soft-spoken. "You can't tell me that sort of stuff. Where d'ye keep your own boats, hey— your schooner, or cutter, or whatever you have? Hey? Answer me that."

McCoy smiled as gently as he spoke. His smile was a caress, an embrace that surrounded the tired mate and sought to draw him into the quietude and rest of McCoy's tranquil soul.

"We have no schooner or cutter," he replied. "And we carry our canoes to the top of the cliff."

"You've got to show me," snorted the mate. "How d'ye get around to the other islands, heh? Tell me that."

"We don't get around. As governor of Pitcairn, I sometimes

go. When I was younger, I was away a great deal—sometimes on the trading schooners, but mostly on the missionary brig. But she's gone now, and we depend on passing vessels. Sometimes we have had as high as six calls in one year. At other times, a year, and even longer, has gone by without one passing ship. Yours is the first in seven months."

"And you mean to tell me—" the mate began.

But Captain Davenport interfered.

"Enough of this. We're losing time. What is to be done, Mr. McCoy?"

The old man turned his brown eyes, sweet as a woman's, shoreward, and both captain and mate followed his gaze around from the lonely rock of Pitcairn to the crew clustering forward and waiting anxiously for the announcement of a decision. McCoy did not hurry. He thought smoothly and slowly, step by step, with the certitude of a mind that was never vexed or outraged by life.

"The wind is light now," he said finally. "There is a heavy current setting to the westward."

"That's what made us fetch to leeward," the captain interrupted, desiring to vindicate his seamanship.

"Yes, that is what fetched you to leeward," McCoy went on. "Well, you can't work up against this current to-day. And if you did, there is no beach. Your ship will be a total loss."

He paused, and captain and mate looked despair at each other.

"But I will tell you what you can do. The breeze will freshen to-night around midnight—see those tails of clouds and that thickness to windward, beyond the point there? That's where she'll come from, out of the southeast, hard. It is three hundred miles to Mangareva. Square away for it. There is a beautiful bed for your ship there."

The mate shook his head.

"Come in to the cabin, and we'll look at the chart," said the captain.

McCoy found a stifling, poisonous atmosphere in the pent cabin. Stray waftures of invisible gases bit his eyes and made them sting. The deck was hotter, almost unbearably hot to his bare feet. The sweat poured out of his body. He looked almost with apprehension about him. This malignant, internal heat was astounding. It was a marvel that the cabin did not burst into flames. He had a feeling as if of being in a huge bake-oven where the heat might at any moment increase tremendously and shrivel him up like a blade of grass.

As he lifted one foot and rubbed the hot sole against the leg of his trousers, the mate laughed in a savage, snarling fashion.

"The anteroom of hell," he said. "Hell herself is right down there under your feet."

"It's hot!" McCoy cried involuntarily, mopping his face with a bandana handkerchief.

"Here's Mangareva," the captain said, bending over the table and pointing to a black speck in the midst of the white blankness of the chart. "And here, in between, is another island. Why not run for that?"

McCoy did not look at the chart.

"That's Crescent Island," he answered. "It is uninhabited, and it is only two or three feet above water. Lagoon, but no entrance. No, Mangareva is the nearest place for your purpose."

"Mangareva it is, then," said Captain Davenport, interrupting the mate's growling objection. "Call the crew aft, Mr. Konig."

The sailors obeyed, shuffling wearily along the deck and painfully endeavoring to make haste. Exhaustion was evident in every movement. The cook came out of his galley to hear, and the cabin-boy hung about near him.

When Captain Davenport had explained the situation and announced his intention of running for Mangareva, an uproar broke out. Against a background of throaty rumbling arose inarticulate cries of rage, with here and there a distinct curse, or word, or phrase. A shrill Cockney voice soared and dominated for a moment, crying: "Gawd! After bein' in 'ell for fifteen days—an' now 'e wants us to sail this floatin' 'ell to sea again!"

The captain could not control them, but McCoy's gentle presence seemed to rebuke and calm them, and the muttering and cursing died away, until the full crew, save here and there an anxious face directed at the captain, yearned dumbly toward the green-clad peaks and beetling coast of Pitcairn.

Soft as a spring zephyr was the voice of McCoy:

"Captain, I thought I heard some of them say they were starving."

"Ay," was the answer, "and so we are. I've had a sea-biscuit and a spoonful of salmon in the last two days. We're on whack. You see, when we discovered the fire, we battened down immediately to suffocate the fire. And then we found how little food there was in the pantry. But it was too late. We didn't dare break out the lazarette. Hungry? I'm just as hungry as they are."

He spoke to the men again, and again the throat-rumbling and cursing arose, their faces convulsed and animal-like with rage. The second and third mates had joined the captain, standing behind him at the break of the poop. Their faces were set and expressionless; they seemed bored, more than anything else, by this mutiny of the crew. Captain Davenport glanced questioningly at his first mate, and that person merely shrugged his shoulders in token of his helplessness.

"You see," the captain said to McCoy, "you can't compel sailors to leave the safe land and go to sea on a burning vessel. She has been their floating coffin for over two weeks now. They are worked out, and starved out, and they've got enough of her. We'll beat up for Pitcairn."

But the wind was light, the *Pyrenees'* bottom was foul, and she could not beat up against the strong westerly current. At the end of two hours she had lost three miles. The sailors worked eagerly, as if by main strength they could compel the *Pyrenees* against the adverse elements. But steadily, port tack and starboard tack, she sagged off to the westward. The captain paced restlessly up and down, pausing occasionally to survey the vagrant smoke-wisps and to trace them back to the portions of the deck from which they sprang. The carpenter was engaged constantly in attempting to locate such places, and, when he succeeded, in calking them tighter and tighter.

"Well, what do you think?" the captain finally asked McCoy, who was watching the carpenter with all a child's interest and curiosity in his eyes.

McCoy looked shoreward, where the land was disappearing in the thickening haze.

"I think it would be better to square away for Mangareva. With that breeze that is coming, you'll be there to-morrow evening."

"But what if the fire breaks out? It is liable to do it any moment."

"Have your boats ready in the falls. The same breeze will carry your boats to Mangareva if the ship burns out from under."

Captain Davenport debated for a moment, and then McCoy heard the question he had not wanted to hear, but which he knew was surely coming.

"I have no chart of Mangareva. On the general chart it is only a fly-speck. I would not know where to look for the entrance into the lagoon. Will you come along and pilot her in for me?"

McCoy's serenity was unbroken.

"Yes, Captain," he said, with the same quiet unconcern with which he would have accepted an invitation to dinner; "I'll go with you to Mangareva."

Again the crew was called aft, and the captain spoke to them from the break of the poop.

"We've tried to work her up, but you see how we've lost ground. She's setting off in a two-knot current. This gentleman is the Honorable McCoy, Chief Magistrate and Governor of Pitcairn Island. He will come along with us to Mangareva. So you see the situation is not so dangerous. He would not make such an offer if he thought he was going to lose his life. Besides, whatever risk there is, if he of his own free will come on board and take it, we can do no less. What do you say for Mangareva?"

This time there was no uproar. McCoy's presence, the surety and calm that seemed to radiate from him, had had its effect. They conferred with one another in low voices. There was little urging. They were virtually unanimous, and they shoved the Cockney out as their spokesman. That worthy was overwhelmed with consciousness of the heroism of himself and his mates, and with flashing eyes he cried:

"By Gawd! if 'e will, we will!"

The crew mumbled its assent and started forward.

"One moment, Captain," McCoy said, as the other was turning to give orders to the mate. "I must go ashore first."

Mr. Konig was thunderstruck, staring at McCoy as if he were a madman.

"Go ashore!" the captain cried. "What for? It will take you three hours to get there in your canoe."

McCoy measured the distance of the land away, and nodded.

"Yes, it is six now. I won't get ashore till nine. The people cannot be assembled earlier than ten. As the breeze freshens up tonight, you can begin to work up against it, and pick me up at daylight tomorrow morning."

"In the name of reason and common sense," the captain burst forth, "what do you want to assemble the people for? Don't you realize that my ship is burning beneath me?"

McCoy was as placid as a summer sea, and the other's anger produced not the slightest ripple upon it.

"Yes, Captain," he cooed in his dove-like voice, "I do realize that your ship is burning. That is why I am going with you to Mangareva. But I must get permission to go with you. It is our custom. It is an important matter when the governor leaves the island. The people's interests are at stake, and so they have the right to vote their permission or refusal. But they will give it, I know that."

"Are you sure?"

"Quite sure."

"Then if you know they will give it, why bother with getting it? Think of the delay—a whole night."

"It is our custom," was the imperturbable reply. "Also, I am the governor, and I must make arrangements for the conduct of the island during my absence."

"But it is only a twenty-four-hour run to Mangareva," the captain objected. "Suppose it took you six times that long to return to windward; that would bring you back by the end of a week."

McCoy smiled his large, benevolent smile.

"Very few vessels come to Pitcairn, and when they do, they are usually from San Francisco or from around the Horn. I shall be fortunate if I get back in six months. I may be away a year, and I may have to go to San Francisco in order to find a vessel that will bring me back. My father once left Pitcairn to be gone three months, and two years passed before he could get back. Then, too, you are short of food. If you have to take to the boats, and the weather comes up bad, you may be days in reaching land. I can bring off two canoe loads of food in the morning. Dried bananas will be best. As the breeze freshens, you beat up against it. The nearer you are, the bigger loads I can bring off. Good-by."

He held out his hand. The captain shook it, and was reluctant to let go. He seemed to cling to it as a drowning sailor clings to a life-buoy.

"How do I know you will come back in the morning?" he asked.

"Yes, that's it!" cried the mate. "How do we know but what he's skinning out to save his own hide?"

McCoy did not speak. He looked at them sweetly and benignantly, and it seemed to them that they received a message from his tremendous certitude of soul.

The captain released his hand, and, with a last sweeping glance that embraced the crew in its benediction, McCoy went over the rail and descended into his canoe.

The wind freshened, and the *Pyrenees,* despite the foulness of her bottom, won half a dozen miles away from the westerly current. At daylight, with Pitcairn three miles to windward, Captain Davenport made out two canoes coming off to him. Again McCoy clambered up the side and dropped over the rail to the hot deck. He was followed by many packages of dried bananas, each package wrapped in dry leaves.

"Now, Captain," he said, "swing the yards and drive for dear life. You see, I am no navigator," he explained a few minutes later, as he stood by the captain aft, the latter with gaze wandering from aloft to overside as he estimated the *Pyrenees'* speed. "You must fetch her to Mangareva. When you have picked up the land, then I will pilot her in. What do you think she is making?"

"Eleven," Captain Davenport answered, with a final glance at the water rushing past.

"Eleven. Let me see, if she keeps up that gait, we'll sight Mangareva between eight and nine o'clock to-morrow morning. I'll have her on the beach by ten, or by eleven at latest. And then your troubles will be all over."

It almost seemed to the captain that the blissful moment had already arrived, such was the persuasive convincingness of McCoy. Captain Davenport had been under the fearful strain of navigating his burning ship for over two weeks, and he was beginning to feel that he had had enough.

A heavier flow of wind struck the back of his neck and whistled by his ears. He measured the weight of it, and looked quickly overside.

"The wind is making all the time," he announced. "The old girl's doing nearer twelve than eleven right now. If this keeps up, we'll be shortening down to-night."

All day the *Pyrenees*, carrying her load of living fire, tore across the foaming sea. By nightfall, royals and topgallantsails were in, and she flew on into the darkness, with great, crested seas roaring after her. The auspicious wind had had its effect, and fore and aft a visible brightening was apparent. In the second dog-watch some careless soul started a song, and by eight bells the whole crew was singing.

Captain Davenport had his blankets brought up and spread on top the house.

"I've forgotten what sleep is," he explained to McCoy. "I'm all in. But give me a call at any time you think necessary."

At three in the morning he was aroused by a gentle tugging at his arm. He sat up quickly, bracing himself against the skylight, stupid yet from his heavy sleep. The wind was thrumming its war-song in the rigging, and a wild sea was buffeting the *Pyrenees*. Amidships she was wallowing first one rail under and then the other, flooding the waist more often than not. McCoy was shouting something he could not hear. He reached out, clutched the other by the shoulder, and drew him close so that his own ear was close to the other's lips.

"It's three o'clock," came McCoy's voice, still retaining its dovelike quality, but curiously muffled, as if from a long way off. "We've run two hundred and fifty. Crescent Island is only thirty miles away, somewhere there dead ahead. There's no lights on it. If we keep running, we'll pile up, and lose ourselves as well as the ship."

"What d' ye think—heave to?"

"Yes; heave to till daylight. It will only put us back four hours."

So the *Pyrenees*, with her cargo of fire, was hove to, bitting the teeth of the gale and fighting and smashing the pounding seas. She was a shell, filled with a conflagration, and on the outside of the shell, clinging precariously, the little motes of men, by pull and haul, helped her in the battle.

"It is most unusual, this gale," McCoy told the captain, in the lee of the cabin. "By rights there should be no gale at this time of the year. But everything about the weather has been unusual. There has been a stoppage of the trades, and now it's howling right out of the trade quarter." He waved his hand into the darkness, as if his vision could dimly penetrate for hundreds of miles. "It is off to the westward. There is something big making off there somewhere—a hurricane or something. We're lucky to be so far to the eastward. But this is only a little blow," he added. "It can't last. I can tell you that much."

By daylight the gale had eased down to normal. But daylight revealed a new danger. It had come on thick. The sea was covered by a fog, or, rather, by a pearly mist that was fog-like in density, in so far as it obstructed vision, but that was no more than a film on the sea, for the sun shot it through and filled it with a glowing radiance.

The deck of the *Pyrenees* was making more smoke than on the preceding day, and the cheerfulness of officers and crew had vanished. In the lee of the galley the cabin-boy could be heard whimpering. It was his first voyage, and the fear of death was at his heart. The captain wandered about like a lost soul, nervously chewing his mustache, scowling, unable to make up his mind what to do.

"What do you think?" he asked, pausing by the side of McCoy, who was making a breakfast off fried bananas and a mug of water.

McCoy finished the last banana, drained the mug, and looked slowly around. In his eyes was a smile of tenderness as he said:

"Well, Captain, we might as well drive as burn. Your decks are not going to hold out forever. They are hotter this morning. You haven't a pair of shoes I can wear? It is getting uncomfortable for my bare feet."

The *Pyrenees* shipped two heavy seas as she was swung off and put once more before it, and the first mate expressed a desire to have all that water down in the hold, if only it could be introduced without taking off the hatches. McCoy ducked his head into the binnacle and watched the course set.

"I'd hold her up some more, Captain," he said. "She's been making drift when hove to."

"I've set it to a point higher already," was the answer. "Isn't that enough?"

"I'd make it two points, Captain. This bit of a blow kicked that westerly current ahead faster than you imagine."

Captain Davenport compromised on a point and a half, and then went aloft, accompanied by McCoy and the first mate, to keep a lookout for land. Sail had been made, so that the *Pyrenees* was doing ten knots. The following sea was dying down rapidly. There was no break in the pearly fog, and by ten o'clock Captain Davenport was growing nervous. All hands were at their stations, ready, at the first warning of land ahead, to spring like fiends to the task of bringing the *Pyrenees* up on the wind. That land ahead, a surf-washed outer reef, would be perilously close when it revealed itself in such a fog.

Another hour passed. The three watchers aloft stared intently into the pearly radiance.

"What if we miss Mangareva?" Captain Davenport asked abruptly.

McCoy, without shifting his gaze, answered softly:

"Why, let her drive, Captain. That is all we can do. All the Paumotus are before us. We can drive for a thousand miles through reefs and atolls. We are bound to fetch up somewhere."

"Then drive it is." Captain Davenport evidenced his intention of descending to the deck. "We've missed Mangareva. God knows where the next land is. I wish I'd held her up that other half-point," he confessed a moment later. "This cursed current plays the devil with a navigator."

"The old navigators called the Paumotus the Dangerous Archipelago," McCoy said, when they had regained the poop. "This very current was partly responsible for that name."

"I was talking with a sailor chap in Sydney, once," said Mr.

Konig. "He'd been trading in the Paumotus. He told me insurance was eighteen per cent. Is that right?"

McCoy smiled and nodded.

"Except that they don't insure," he explained. "The owners write off twenty per cent of the cost of their schooners each year."

"My God!" Captain Davenport groaned. "That makes the life of a schooner only five years!" He shook his head sadly, murmuring, "Bad waters! bad waters!"

Again they went into the cabin to consult the big general chart; but the poisonous vapors drove them coughing and gasping on deck.

"Here is Moerenhout Island." Captain Davenport pointed it out on the chart, which he had spread on the house. "It can't be more than a hundred miles to leeward."

"A hundred and ten." McCoy shook his head doubtfully. "It might be done, but it is very difficult. I might beach her, and then again I might put her on the reef. A bad place, a very bad place."

"We'll take the chance," was Captain Davenport's decision, as he set about working out the course.

Sail was shortened early in the afternoon, to avoid running past in the night; and in the second dog-watch the crew manifested its regained cheerfulness. Land was so very near, and their troubles would be over in the morning.

But morning broke clear, with a blazing tropic sun. The southeast trade had swung around to the eastward, and was driving the *Pyrenees* through the water at an eight-knot clip. Captain Davenport worked up his dead reckoning, allowing generously for drift, and announced Moerenhout Island to be not more than ten miles off. The *Pyrenees* sailed the ten miles; she sailed ten miles more; and the lookouts at the three mastheads saw naught but the naked, sun-washed sea.

"But the land is there, I tell you," Captain Davenport shouted to them from the poop.

McCoy smiled soothingly, but the captain glared about him like a madman, fetched his sextant, and took a chronometer sight.

"I knew I was right," he almost shouted, when he had worked up the observation. "Twenty-one, fifty-five, south; one-thirty-six, two, west. There you are. We're eight miles to windward yet. What did you make it out, Mr. Konig?"

The first mate glanced at his own figures, and said in a low voice:

"Twenty-one, fifty-five all right; but my longitude's one-thirty-six, forty-eight. That puts us considerably to leeward—"

But Captain Davenport ignored his figures with so contemptuous a silence as to make Mr. Konig grit his teeth and curse savagely under his breath.

"Keep her off," the captain ordered the man at the wheel. "Three points—steady there, as she goes!"

Then he returned to his figures and worked them over. The sweat poured from his face. He chewed his mustache, his lips, and his pencil, staring at the figures as a man might at a ghost. Suddenly, with a fierce, muscular outburst, he crumpled the scribbled paper in his fist and crushed it under foot. Mr. Konig grinned vindictively and turned away, while Captain Davenport leaned against the cabin and for half an hour spoke no word, contenting himself with gazing to leeward with an expression of musing hopelessness on his face.

"Mr. McCoy," he broke silence abruptly. "The chart indicates a group of islands, but not how many, off there to the north'ard, or nor'-nor'westward, about forty miles—the Acteon Islands. What about them?"

"There are four, all low," McCoy answered. "First to the southeast is Matuerui—no people, no entrance to the lagoon. Then comes Tenarunga. There used to be about a dozen people there, but they may be all gone now. Anyway, there is no entrance for a ship—only a boat entrance, with a fathom of water. Vehauga and Teua-raro are the other two. No entrances, no people, very low. There is no bed for the *Pyrenees* in that group. She would be a total wreck."

"Listen to that!" Captain Davenport was frantic. "No people! No entrances! What in the devil are islands good for?

"Well, then," he barked suddenly, like an excited terrier, "the chart gives a whole mess of islands off to the nor'west. What about them? What one has an entrance where I can lay my ship?"

McCoy calmly considered. He did not refer to the chart. All these islands, reefs, shoals, lagoons, entrances, and distances were marked on the chart of his memory. He knew them as the city dweller knows his buildings, streets, and alleys.

"Papakena and Vanavana are off there to the westward, or west-nor'westward a hundred miles and a bit more," he said. "One is uninhabited, and I heard that the people on the other had gone off to Cadmus Island. Anyway, neither lagoon has an entrance. Ahunui is another hundred miles on to the nor'west. No entrance, no people."

"Well, forty miles beyond them are two islands?" Captain Davenport queried, raising his head from the chart.

McCoy shook his head.

"Paros and Manuhungi—no entrances, no people. Nengo-Nengo is forty miles beyond them, in turn, and it has no people and no entrance. But there is Hao Island. It is just the place. The lagoon is thirty miles long and five miles wide. There are plenty of people. You can usually find water. And any ship in the world can go through the entrance."

He ceased and gazed solicitously at Captain Davenport, who, bending over the chart with a pair of dividers in hand, had just emitted a low groan.

"Is there any lagoon with an entrance anywhere nearer than Hao Island?" he asked.

"No, Captain; that is the nearest."

"Well, it's three hundred and forty miles." Captain Davenport was speaking very slowly, with decision. "I won't risk the responsibility of all these lives. I'll wreck her on the Acteons. And she's a good ship, too," he added regretfully, after altering the course, this time making more allowance than ever for the westerly current.

An hour later the sky was overcast. The southeast trade still held, but the ocean was a checker-board of squalls.

"We'll be there by one o'clock," Captain Davenport announced confidently. "By two o'clock at the outside. McCoy, you put her ashore on the one where the people are."

The sun did not appear again, nor, at one o'clock, was any land to be seen. Captain Davenport looked astern at the *Pyrenees'* canting wake.

"Good Lord!" he cried. "An easterly current! Look at that!"

Mr. Konig was incredulous. McCoy was noncommittal, though he said that in the Paumotus there was no reason why it should not be an easterly current. A few minutes later a squall robbed the *Pyrenees* temporarily of all her wind, and she was left rolling heavily in the trough.

"Where's that deep lead? Over with it, you there!" Captain Davenport held the lead-line and watched it sag off to the northeast. "There, look at that! Take hold of it for yourself."

McCoy and the mate tried it, and felt the line thrumming and vibrating savagely to the grip of the tidal stream.

"A four-knot current," said Mr. Konig.

"An easterly current instead of a westerly," said Captain Davenport, glaring accusingly at McCoy, as if to cast the blame for it upon him.

"That is one of the reasons, Captain, for insurance being eighteen per cent in these waters," McCoy answered cheerfully. "You never can tell. The currents are always changing. There was a man who wrote books, I forget his name, in the yacht *Casco*. He missed Takaroa by thirty miles and fetched Tikei, all because of the shifting currents. You are up to windward now, and you'd better keep off a few points."

"But how much has this current set me?" the captain demanded irately. "How am I to know how much to keep off?"

"I don't know, Captain," McCoy said with great gentleness.

The wind returned, and the *Pyrenees*, her deck smoking and shimmering in the bright gray light, ran off dead to leeward. Then she worked back, port tack and starboard tack, crisscrossing her track, combing the sea for the Acteon Islands, which the masthead lookouts failed to sight.

Captain Davenport was beside himself. His rage took the form of sullen silence, and he spent the afternoon in pacing the poop or leaning against the weather-shrouds. At nightfall, without even consulting McCoy, he squared away and headed into the northwest. Mr. Konig, surreptitiously consulting chart and binnacle, and McCoy, openly and innocently consulting the binnacle, knew that they were running for Hao Island. By midnight the squalls ceased, and the stars came out. Captain Davenport was cheered by the promise of a clear day.

"I'll get an observation in the morning," he told McCoy, "though what my latitude is, is a puzzler. But I'll use the Sumner method, and settle that. Do you know the Sumner line?"

And thereupon he explained it in detail to McCoy.

The day proved clear, the trade blew steadily out of the east, and the *Pyrenees* just as steadily logged her nine knots. Both the captain and mate worked out the position on a Sumner line, and agreed, and at noon agreed again, and verified the morning sights by the noon sights.

"Another twenty-four hours and we'll be there," Captain Davenport assured McCoy. "It's a miracle the way the old girl's decks hold out. But they can't last. They can't last. Look at them smoke, more and more every day. Yet it was a tight deck to begin with, fresh-calked in 'Frisco. I was surprised when the fire first broke out and we battened down. Look at that!"

He broke off to gaze with dropped jaw at a spiral of smoke that coiled and twisted in the lee of the mizzenmast twenty feet above the deck.

"Now, how did that get there?" he demanded indignantly.

Beneath it there was no smoke. Crawling up from the deck, sheltered from the wind by the mast, by some freak it took form and visibility at that height. It writhed away from the mast, and for a moment overhung the captain like some threatening portent. The next moment the wind whisked it away, and the captain's jaw returned to place.

"As I was saying, when we first battened down, I was surprised. It was a tight deck, yet it leaked smoke like a sieve. And we've calked and calked ever since. There must be tremendous pressure underneath to drive so much smoke through."

That afternoon the sky became overcast again, and squally, drizzly weather set in. The wind shifted back and forth between southeast and northeast, and at midnight the *Pyrenees* was caught aback by a sharp squall from the southwest, from which point the wind continued to blow intermittently.

"We won't make Hao until ten or eleven," Captain Davenport complained at seven in the morning, when the fleeting promise of the sun had been erased by hazy cloud masses in the eastern sky. And the next moment he was plaintively demanding, "And what are the currents doing?"

Lookouts at the mastheads could report no land, and the day passed in drizzling calms and violent squalls. By nightfall a heavy sea began to make from the west. The barometer had fallen to 29.50. There was no wind, and still the ominous sea continued to increase. Soon the *Pyrenees* was rolling madly in the huge waves that marched in an unending procession from out of the darkness of the west. Sail was shortened as fast as both watches could work, and, when the tired crew had finished, its grumbling and complaining voices, peculiarly animal-like and menacing, could be heard in the darkness. Once the starboard watch was called aft to lash down and make secure, and the men openly advertised their sullenness and unwillingness. Every slow movement was a protest and a threat. The atmosphere was moist and sticky like mucilage, and in the absence of wind all hands seemed to pant and gasp for air. The sweat stood out on faces and bare arms, and Captain Davenport for one, his face more gaunt and care-worn than ever, and his eyes troubled and staring, was oppressed by a feeling of impending calamity.

"It's off to the westward," McCoy said encouragingly. "At worst, we'll be only on the edge of it."

But Captain Davenport refused to be comforted, and by the light of a lantern read up the chapter in his *Epitome* that related to the strategy of shipmasters in cyclonic storms. From somewhere amidships the silence was broken by a low whimpering from the cabin-boy.

"Oh, shut up!" Captain Davenport yelled suddenly and with such force as to startle every man on board and to frighten the offender into a wild wail of terror.

"Mr. Konig," the captain said in a voice that trembled with rage and nerves, "will you kindly step for'ard and stop that brat's mouth with a deck mop?"

But it was McCoy who went forward, and in a few minutes had the boy comforted and asleep.

Shortly before daybreak the first breath of air began to move from out the southeast, increasing swiftly to a stiff and stiffer breeze. All hands were on deck waiting for what might be behind it.

"We're all right now, Captain," said McCoy, standing close to his shoulder. "The hurricane is to the west'ard, and we are south of it. This breeze is the in-suck. It won't blow any harder. You can begin to put sail on her."

"But what's the good? Where shall I sail? This is the second day without observations, and we should have sighted Hao Island yesterday morning. Which way does it bear, north, south, east, or what? Tell me that, and I'll make sail in a jiffy."

"I am no navigator, Captain," McCoy said in his mild way.

"I used to think I was one," was the retort, "before I got into these Paumotus."

At mid-day the cry of "Breakers ahead!" was heard from the lookout. The *Pyrenees* was kept off, and sail after sail was loosed and sheeted home. The *Pyrenees* was sliding through the water and fighting a current that threatened to set her down upon the breakers. Officers and men were working like mad, cook and cabin-boy, Captain Davenport himself, and McCoy all lending a hand. It was a close shave. It was a low shoal, a bleak and perilous place over which the seas broke unceasingly, where no man could live, and on which not even sea-birds could rest. The *Pyrenees* was swept within a hundred yards of it before the wind carried her clear, and at this moment the panting crew, its work done, burst out in a torrent of curses upon the head of McCoy—of McCoy who had come on board, and proposed to run to Mangareva, and lured them all away from the safety of Pitcairn Island to certain destruction in this baffling and terrible stretch of sea. But McCoy's tranquil soul was undisturbed. He smiled at them with simple and gracious benevolence, and, somehow, the exalted goodness of him seemed to penetrate to their dark and sombre souls, shaming them, and from very shame stilling the curses vibrating in their throats.

"Bad waters! bad waters!" Captain Davenport was murmuring as his ship forged clear; but he broke off abruptly to gaze at the shoal which should have been dead astern, but which was already on the *Pyrenees'* weather-quarter and working up rapidly to windward.

He sat down and buried his face in his hands. And the first mate saw, and McCoy saw, and the crew saw, what he had seen. South of the shoal an easterly current had set them down upon it; north of the shoal an equally swift westerly current had clutched the ship and was sweeping her away.

"I've heard of these Paumotus before," the captain groaned, lifting his blanched face from his hands. "Captain Moyendale told me about them after losing his ship on them. And I laughed at him behind his back. God forgive me, I laughed at him. What shoal is that?" he broke off, to ask McCoy.

"I don't know, Captain."

"Why don't you know?"

"Because I never saw it before, and because I have never heard of it. I do know that it is not charted. These waters have never been thoroughly surveyed."

"Then you don't know where we are?"

"No more than you do," McCoy said gently.

At four in the afternoon cocoanut-trees were sighted, apparently growing out of the water. A little later the low land of an atoll was raised above the sea.

"I know where we are now, Captain." McCoy lowered the glasses from his eyes. "That's Resolution Island. We are forty miles beyond Hao Island, and the wind is in our teeth."

"Get ready to beach her then. Where's the entrance?"

"There's only a canoe passage. But now that we know where we are, we can run for Barclay de Tolley. It is only one hundred and twenty miles from here, due nor'-nor'west. With this breeze we can be there by nine o'clock to-morrow morning."

Captain Davenport consulted the chart and debated with himself.

"If we wreck her here," McCoy added, "we'd have to make the run to Barclay de Tolley in the boats just the same."

The captain gave his orders, and once more the *Pyrenees* swung off for another run across the inhospitable sea.

And the middle of the next afternoon saw despair and mutiny on her smoking deck. The current had accelerated, the wind had slackened, and the *Pyrenees* had sagged off to the west. The lookout sighted Barclay de Tolley to the eastward, barely visible from the masthead, and vainly and for hours the *Pyrenees* tried to beat up to it. Ever, like a mirage, the cocoanut-trees hovered on the horizon, visible only from the masthead. From the deck they were hidden by the bulge of the world.

Again Captain Davenport consulted McCoy and the chart. Makemo lay seventy-five miles to the southwest. Its lagoon was thirty miles long, and its entrance was excellent. When Captain Davenport gave his orders, the crew refused duty. They announced that they had had enough of hell-fire under their feet. There was the land. What if the ship could not make it? They could make it in the boats. Let her burn, then. Their lives amounted to something to them. They had served faithfully the ship, now they were going to serve themselves.

They sprang to the boats, brushing the second and third mates out of the way, and proceeded to swing the boats out and to prepare to lower away. Captain Davenport and the first mate, revolvers in hand, were advancing to the break of the poop, when McCoy, who had climbed on top of the cabin, began to speak.

He spoke to the sailors, and at the first sound of his dovelike, cooing voice they paused to hear. He extended to them his own ineffable serenity and peace. His soft voice and simple thoughts flowed out to them in a magic stream, soothing them against their wills. Long forgotten things came back to them, and some remembered lullaby songs of childhood and the content and rest of the mother's arm at the end of the day. There was no more trouble, no more danger, no more irk, in all the world. Everything was as it should be, and it was only a matter of course that they should turn their backs upon the land and put to sea once more with hell-fire hot beneath their feet.

McCoy spoke simply; but it was not what he spoke. It was his personality that spoke more eloquently than any word he could utter. It was an alchemy of soul occultly subtle and profoundly deep—a mysterious emanation of the spirit, seductive, sweetly humble, and terribly imperious. It was illumination in the dark crypts of their souls, a compulsion of purity and gentleness vastly greater than that which resided in the shining, death-spitting revolvers of the officers.

The men wavered reluctantly where they stood, and those who had loosed the turns made them fast again. Then one, and then another, and then all of them, began to sidle awkwardly away.

McCoy's face was beaming with childlike pleasure as he descended from the top of the cabin. There was no trouble. For that matter there had been no trouble averted. There never had been any trouble, for there was no place for such in the blissful world in which he lived.

"You hypnotized 'em," Mr. Konig grinned at him, speaking in a low voice.

"Those boys are good," was the answer. "Their hearts are good. They have had a hard time, and they have worked hard, and they will work hard to the end."

Mr. Konig had no time to reply. His voice was ringing out orders, the sailors were springing to obey, and the *Pyrenees* was paying slowly off from the wind until her bow should point in the direction of Makemo.

The wind was very light, and after sundown almost ceased. It was insufferably warm, and fore and aft men sought vainly to sleep. The deck was too hot to lie upon, and poisonous vapors, oozing through the seams, crept like evil spirits over the ship, stealing into the nostrils and windpipes of the unwary and causing fits of sneezing and coughing. The stars blinked lazily in the dim vault overhead; and the full moon, rising in the east, touched with its light the myriads of wisps and threads and spidery films of smoke that intertwined and writhed and twisted along the deck, over the rails, and up the masts and shrouds.

"Tell me," Captain Davenport said, rubbing his smarting eyes, "what happened with that *Bounty* crowd after they reached Pitcairn? The account I read said they burnt the *Bounty,* and that they were not discovered until many years later. But what happened in the meantime? I've always been curious to know. They were men with their necks in the rope. There were some native men, too. And then there were women. That made it look like trouble right from the jump."

"There was trouble," McCoy answered. "They were bad men. They quarrelled about the women right away. One of the mutineers, Williams, lost his wife. All the women were Tahitian women. His wife fell from the cliffs when hunting sea-birds. Then he took the wife of one of the native men away from him. All the native men were made very angry by this, and they killed off nearly all the mutineers. Then the mutineers that escaped killed off all the native men. The women helped. And the natives killed each other. Everybody killed everybody. They were terrible men.

"Timiti was killed by two other natives while they were combing his hair in friendship. The white men had sent them to do it. Then the white men killed them. The wife of Tullaloo killed him in a cave because she wanted a white man for husband. They were very wicked. God had hidden His face from them. At the end of two years all the native men were murdered, and all the white men except four. They were Young, John Adams, McCoy, who was my great-grandfather, and Quintal. He was a very bad man, too. Once, just because his wife did not catch enough fish for him, he bit off her ear."

"They were a bad lot!" Mr. Konig exclaimed.

"Yes, they were very bad," McCoy agreed and went on serenely cooing of the blood and lust of his iniquitous ancestry. "My great-grandfather escaped murder in order to die by his own hand. He made a still and manufactured alcohol from the roots of the ti-plant. Quintal was his chum, and they got drunk together all the time. At last McCoy got delirium tremens, tied a rock to his neck, and jumped into the sea.

"Quintal's wife, the one whose ear he bit off, also got killed by falling from the cliffs. Then Quintal went to Young and demanded his wife, and went to Adams and demanded his wife. Adams and Young were afraid of Quintal. They knew he would kill them. So they killed him, the two of them together, with a hatchet. Then Young died. And that was about all the trouble they had."

"I should say so," Captain Davenport snorted. "There was nobody left to kill."

"You see, God had hidden His face," McCoy said.

By morning no more than a faint air was blowing from the eastward, and, unable to make appreciable southing by it, Captain Davenport hauled up full-and-by on the port track. He was afraid of that terrible westerly current which had cheated him out of so many ports of refuge. All day the calm continued, and all night, while the sailors, on a short ration of dried banana, were grumbling. Also, they were growing weak and complaining of stomach pains caused by the straight banana diet. All day the current swept the *Pyrenees* to the westward, while there was no wind to bear her south. In the middle of the first dogwatch, cocoanut-trees were sighted due south, their tufted heads rising above the water and marking the low-lying atoll beneath.

"That is Taenga Island," McCoy said. "We need a breeze to-night, or else we'll miss Makemo."

"What's become of the southeast trade?" the captain demanded. "Why don't it blow? What's the matter?"

"It is the evaporation from the big lagoons—there are so many of them," McCoy explained. "The evaporation upsets the whole system of trades. It even causes the wind to back up and blow gales from the southwest. This is the Dangerous Archipelago, Captain."

Captain Davenport faced the old man, opened his mouth, and was about to curse, but paused and refrained. McCoy's presence was a rebuke to the blasphemies that stirred in his brain and trembled in his larynx. McCoy's influence had been growing during the many days they had been together. Captain Davenport was an autocrat of the sea, fearing no man, never bridling his tongue, and now he found himself unable to curse in the presence of this old man with the feminine brown eyes and the voice of a dove. When he realized this, Captain Davenport experienced a distinct shock. This old man was merely the seed of McCoy, of McCoy of the *Bounty*, the mutineer fleeing from the hemp that waited him in England, the McCoy who was a power for evil in the early days of blood and lust and violent death on Pitcairn Island.

Captain Davenport was not religious, yet in that moment he felt a mad impulse to cast himself at the other's feet—and to say he knew not what. It was an emotion that so deeply stirred him, rather than a coherent thought, and he was aware in some vague way of his own unworthiness and smallness in the presence of this other man who possessed the simplicity of a child and the gentleness of a woman.

Of course he could not so humble himself before the eyes of his officers and men. And yet the anger that had prompted the blasphemy still raged in him. He suddenly smote the cabin with his clenched hand and cried:

"Look here, old man, I won't be beaten. These Paumotus have cheated and tricked me and made a fool of me. I refuse to be beaten. I am going to drive this ship, and drive and drive and drive clear through the Paumotus to China but what I find a bed for her. If every man deserts, I'll stay by her. I'll show the Paumotus. They can't fool me. She's a good girl, and I'll stick by her as long as there's a plank to stand on. You hear me?"

"And I'll stay with you, Captain," McCoy said.

During the night, light, baffling airs blew out of the south, and the frantic captain, with his cargo of fire, watched and measured his westward drift and went off by himself at times to curse softly so that McCoy should not hear.

Daylight showed more palms growing out of the water to the south.

"That's the leeward point of Makemo," McCoy said. "Katiu is only a few miles to the west. We may make that."

But the current, sucking between the two islands, swept them to the northwest, and at one in the afternoon they saw the palms of Katiu rise above the sea and sink back into the sea again.

A few minutes later, just as the captain had discovered that a new current from the northeast had gripped the *Pyrenees*, the masthead lookouts raised cocoanut palms in the northwest.

"It is Raraka," said McCoy. "We won't make it without wind. The current is drawing us down to the southwest. But we must watch out. A few miles farther on a current flows north and turns in a circle to the northwest. This will sweep us away from Fakarava, and Fakarava is the place for the *Pyrenees* to find her bed."

"They can sweep all they da—all they well please," Captain

Davenport remarked with heat. "We'll find a bed for her some-where just the same."

But the situation on the *Pyrenees* was reaching a culmination. The deck was so hot that it seemed an increase of a few degrees would cause it to burst into flames. In many places even the heavy-soled shoes of the men were no protection, and they were compelled to step lively to avoid scorching their feet. The smoke had increased and grown more acrid. Every man on board was suffering from inflamed eyes, and they coughed and strangled like a crew of tuberculosis patients. In the afternoon the boats were swung out and equipped. The last several packages of dried bananas were stored in them, as well as the instruments of the officers. Captain Davenport even put the chronometer into the longboat, fearing the blowing up of the deck at any moment.

All night this apprehension weighed heavily on all, and in the first morning light, with hollow eyes and ghastly faces, they stared at one another as if in surprise that the *Pyrenees* still held together and that they still were alive.

Walking rapidly at times, and even occasionally breaking into an undignified hop-skip-and-run, Captain Davenport inspected his ship's deck.

"It is a matter of hours now, if not of minutes," he announced on his return to the poop.

The cry of land came down from the masthead. From the deck the land was invisible, and McCoy went aloft, while the captain took advantage of the opportunity to curse some of the bitterness out of his heart. But the cursing was suddenly stopped by a dark line on the water which he sighted to the northeast. It was not a squall, but a regular breeze—the dis-rupted trade-wind, eight points out of its direction but resuming business once more.

"Hold her up, Captain," McCoy said as soon as he reached the poop. "That's the easterly point of Fakarava, and we'll go in through the passage full-tilt, the wind abeam, and every sail drawing."

At the end of an hour, the cocoanut-trees and the low-lying land were visible from the deck. The feeling that the end of the *Pyrenees*' resistance was imminent weighed heavily on everybody. Captain Davenport had the three boats lowered and dropped short astern, a man in each to keep them apart. The *Pyrenees* closely skirted the shore, the surf-whitened atoll a bare two cable-lengths away.

"Get ready to wear her, Captain," McCoy warned.

And a minute later the land parted, exposing a narrow passage and the lagoon beyond, a great mirror, thirty miles in length and a third as broad.

"Now, Captain."

For the last time the yards of the *Pyrenees* swung around as she obeyed the wheel and headed into the passage. The turns had scarcely been made, and nothing had been coiled down, when the men and mates swept back to the poop in panic terror. Nothing had happened, yet they averred that something was going to happen. They could not tell why. They merely knew that it was about to happen. McCoy started forward to take up his position on the bow in order to con the vessel in; but the captain gripped his arm and whirled him around.

"Do it from here," he said. "That deck's not safe. What's the matter?" he demanded the next instant. "We're standing still."

McCoy smiled.

"You are bucking a seven-knot current, Captain," he said. "That is the way the full ebb runs out of this passage."

At the end of another hour the *Pyrenees* had scarcely gained her length, but the wind freshened and she began to forge ahead.

"Better get into the boats, some of you," Captain Davenport commanded.

His voice was still ringing, and the men were just beginning to move in obedience, when the amidship deck of the *Pyrenees,* in a mass of flame and smoke, was flung upward into the sails and rigging, part of it remaining there and the rest falling into the sea. The wind being abeam, was what had saved the men crowded aft. They made a blind rush to gain the boats, but McCoy's voice, carrying its convincing message of vast calm and endless time, stopped them.

"Take it easy," he was saying. "Everything is all right. Pass that boy down somebody, please."

The man at the wheel had forsaken it in a funk, and Captain Davenport had leaped and caught the spokes in time to prevent the ship from yawing in the current and going ashore.

"Better take charge of the boats," he said to Mr. Konig. "Tow one of them short, right under the quarter. . . . When I go over, it'll be on the jump."

Mr. Konig hesitated, then went over the rail and lowered himself into the boat.

"Keep her off half a point, Captain."

Captain Davenport gave a start. He had thought he had the ship to himself.

"Ay, ay; half a point it is," he answered.

Amidships the *Pyrenees* was an open, flaming furnace, out of which poured an immense volume of smoke which rose high above the masts and completely hid the forward part of the ship. McCoy, in the shelter of the mizzen-shrouds, continued his difficult task of conning the ship through the intricate channel. The fire was working aft along the deck from the seat of explosion, while the soaring tower of canvas on the mainmast went up and vanished in a sheet of flame. Forward, though they could not see them, they knew that the head-sails were still drawing.

"If only she don't burn all her canvas off before she makes inside," the captain groaned.

"She'll make it," McCoy assured him with supreme confidence. "There is plenty of time. She is bound to make it. And once inside, we'll put her before it; that will keep the smoke away from us and hold back the fire from working aft."

A tongue of flame sprang up the mizzen, reached hungrily for the lowest tier of canvas, missed it, and vanished. From aloft a burning shred of rope-stuff fell square on the back of Captain Davenport's neck. He acted with the celerity of one stung by a bee as he reached up and brushed the offending fire from his skin.

"How is she heading, Captain?"

"Nor'west by west."

"Keep her west-nor'west."

Captain Davenport put the wheel up and steadied her.

"West by north, Captain."

"West by north she is."

"And now west."

Slowly, point by point, as she entered the lagoon, the *Pyrenees* described the circle that put her before the wind; and point by point, with all the calm certitude of a thousand years of time to spare, McCoy chanted the changing course.

"Another point, Captain."

"A point it is."

Captain Davenport whirled several spokes over, suddenly reversing and coming back one to check her.

"Steady."

"Steady she is—right on it."

Despite the fact that the wind was now astern, the heat was so intense that Captain Davenport was compelled to steal sidelong glances into the binnacle, letting go the wheel, now with one hand, now with the other, to rub or shield his blistering cheeks. McCoy's beard was crinkling and shrivelling and the smell of it, strong in the other's nostrils, compelled him to look toward McCoy with sudden solicitude. Captain Davenport was letting go the spokes alternately with his hands in order to rub their blistering backs against his trousers. Every sail on the mizzen-mast vanished in a rush of flame, compelling the two men to crouch and shield their faces.

"Now," said McCoy, stealing a glance ahead at the low shore, "four points up, Captain, and let her drive."

Shreds and patches of burning rope and canvas were falling about them and upon them. The tarry smoke from a smouldering piece of rope at the captain's feet set him off into a violent coughing fit, during which he still clung to the spokes.

The *Pyrenees* struck, her bow lifted, and she ground ahead gently to a stop. A shower of burning fragments, dislodged by the shock, fell about them. The ship moved ahead again and struck a second time. She crushed the fragile coral under her keel, drove on, and struck a third time.

"Hard over," said McCoy. "Hard over?" he questioned gently, a minute later.

"She won't answer," was the reply.

"All right. She is swinging around." McCoy peered over the side. "Soft, white sand. Couldn't ask better. A beautiful bed."

As the *Pyrenees* swung around her stern away from the wind, a fearful blast of smoke and flame poured aft. Captain Davenport deserted the wheel in blistering agony. He reached the painter of the boat that lay under the quarter, then looked for McCoy, who was standing aside to let him go down.

"You first," the captain cried, gripping him by the shoulder and almost throwing him over the rail. But the flame and smoke were too terrible, and he followed hard after McCoy, both men wriggling on the rope and sliding down into the boat together. A sailor in the bow, without waiting for orders, slashed the painter through with his sheath-knife. The oars, poised in readiness, bit into the water, and the boat shot away.

"A beautiful bed, Captain," McCoy murmured, looking back.

"Ay, a beautiful bed, and all thanks to you," was the answer.

The three boats pulled away for the white beach of pounded coral, beyond which, on the edge of a cocoanut grove, could be seen a half-dozen grass-houses, and a score or more of excited natives, gazing wide-eyed at the conflagration that had come to land.

The boats grounded and they stepped out on the white beach.

"And now," said McCoy, "I must see about getting back to Pitcairn."